MARDUKITE MASTER COURSE
ACADEMY LECTURES
VOL. 1

MAGICK & MYSTICISM

Titles in this series by Joshua Free:
Vol.1 – Magick & Mysticism
Vol.2 – Druids, Elves & Dragons
Vol.3 – Mesopotamian Tradition
Vol.4 – Mardukite Systemology

Mardukite Research Library Catlogue No. "MMC-1A"

Based on the Lectures by Joshua Free for the
Mardukite Master Course given during September 2020
excerpted from *The Complete Mardukite Master Course*

Every effort has been given to match wording and inflection for lecture transcripts based on the recordings made by Mardukite Academy of Systemology

Published from
Mardukite Borsippa HQ, San Luis Valley, Colorado

cum superiorum privilegio veniaque

The Founding Church of Mardukite Zuism,
Mardukite Academy & Systemology Society

MARDUKITE ACADEMY – COLLECTOR'S EDITION

MARDUKITE MASTER COURSE ACADEMY LECTURES VOL. 1

MAGICK & MYSTICISM

Based on the Lectures
by Joshua Free

© 2022, JOSHUA FREE

ISBN : 979-8-218-01056-0

No part of this publication may be reproduced in any form or by any means, electronic or mechanical, including photocopying, recording, or any information storage or retrieval system, without permission from the publisher. This book is not intended to substitute medical treatment or professional advice.

*The Mardukite Academy Lectures
given during September 2020
for Academy Grade-I Route-A
of the Mardukite Master Course
regarding Magick & Mysticism.*

Mardukite Academy Collector's Edition—*June 2022*
mardukite.com

The _Original_ Master Course Lectures

Commemorating his silver anniversary and drawing from 25 years of experiential esoteric research and underground literary developments, world-renowned mystic philosopher and prodigious occult author, Joshua Free, provides the professional qualifications necessary for "mastering" upper-level understanding of his collected works in the same way that an artist "masters" their craft. Nothing is held back in this surprisingly candid presentation of materials.

This is volume one of a four-part series, providing a serious Seeker with full transcripts to 12 of the 48 Academy Lectures previously published in the mega-anthology "Complete Mardukite Master Course."

Here you will find an insightful tome demonstrating a refreshing approach to understanding magick, the mystical arts and occult sciences in the 21st century.

Although recent years have seen an advancement in the work, all publications by Joshua Free, written and published between 1995 and 2019, pertain to a singular continuum of complete instruction divided into three knowledge tiers or "Grades." A complete library collection of all "core material" described in the "Mardukite Master Course" was also reissued in four different Master Edition textbooks: "The Great Magickal Arcanum," "Merlyn's Complete Book of Druidism," "Necronomicon: The Complete Anunnaki Legacy" and "The Systemology Handbook" – totaling 3,600 pages in all.

Now YOU can experience the legendary "Master Course" from anywhere in the Universe, exactly as given in-person by Joshua Free to the "Mardukite Academy of Systemology" in September 2020.

THE GRADE-I ROUTE-A ACADEMY LECTURES

INTRODUCTIONS

Introducing the Mardukite Master Course . . . 9

Materials of the Mardukite Master Course . . . 17

Mardukite Master Course Training Schedule . . . 19

Introducing Grade-I Route-A Materials . . . 21

THE ACADEMY LECTURES (GRADE-I ROUTE-A)

1—Course Introduction (*Sept. 21, 2020*) . . . 24

2—Introducing the Materials (*Sept. 21, 2020*) . . . 35

3—The Great Magickal Arcanum (*Sept. 21, 2020*) . . . 47

4—Mastering Magic (*Sept. 21, 2020*) . . . 59

5—The Magic School (*Sept. 22, 2020*) . . . 71

6—Fundamentals of Magic (*Sept. 22, 2020*) . . . 84

7—A History of Magic (*Sept. 22, 2020*) . . . 98

8—Basic Magic Tech (*Sept. 22, 2020*) . . . 111

9—Magical Training (*Sept. 22, 2020*) . . . 124

10—Mind Tech (*Sept. 22, 2020*) . . . 138

11—Magical Elements (*Sept. 22, 2020*) . . . 151

12—Elemental Tech (*Sept. 22, 2020*) . . . 164

APPENDIX

Suggested Reading and Additional Materials . . . 177

INTRODUCING THE
MARDUKITE MASTER COURSE

The single most purpose of our *Mardukite Master Course* is to ensure, certify and provide professional qualifications for "mastering" an understanding of the materials in the same way that an artist "masters" their craft. The complete *Mardukite Master Course* spans three *Grades* of knowledge and is given only to those *Seekers* that first properly worked through all three *Grades*, and may then be rightfully considered *Masters* of this knowledge. Extents of such "mastery" should prove readily obvious (objectively), lending to increased qualities of *Self-Actualization*, personal leadership and the certainty to manage and instruct *Mardukite Groups*.

Current works available by Joshua Free—written and published between 1995 and 2019—all pertain to a singular stream of complete instruction that is divided into three *Grades* or knowledge tiers. The *Mardukite Master Course* is intended to grant a clear unification of material presented across all three *Grades* under the banner of "Mardukite Systemology," which is also the name given to *Grade-III*. The two are interconnected (*Grade-III* and the *Master Course*); hence the complete *Mardukite Master Course* is only delivered to *Seekers* at the completion of *Grade-III*. There are "higher" *Grades* within the domain of "NexGen Systemology," but the *Mardukite Master Course* successfully covers all specifically "Mardukite Master" *Grades*: I, II and III.

It is important to clarify what we mean by *Grades* and distinguish the materials that pertain to each. In most instances, instruction for these *Grades*—as delivered in the materials (books) over the past 25 years—was all self-administered; meaning it has been explored independent of properly structured groups or trained instructors. In the past, *Seekers* selected a volume at random, had at it on their own for a while, then walked away with whatever level of understanding might be attained, even if severely fragmented. Most are unaware that the works—no matter the theme—are all tied together. They are divided as follows:

GRADE-I	Western Magical Tradition ("Magick")
GRADE-II	Ancient Mystery School of Mesopotamia
GRADE-III	Futurist/NexGen Mardukite Systemology

It can be said that the *Grades* are all a part of a single continuum—one which is explored in a "reverse engineering" style in order to provide the greatest certainty for effective workable future applications that will advance the spiritual evolution of the *Human Condition*, particularly the *Self* that is participating in and experiencing a co-creation of the Physical Universe and a continued existence of its conditions. As a single continuum, the *Grades* do actually overlap on many points—and often times these "bridges" between levels of understanding are what we are highlighting profusely for our *Mardukite Master Course*. This preferred approach—treating the universal knowledge and its records as a single wholeness rather than an emphasis on individual parts—developed after many years of experiment and discovery.

Direction of the *Mardukite Master Course* loosely follows a chronological pathway charted by Joshua Free from 1995 through 2019—meaning: from the release of the first "Merlyn Stone" *Grade-I* discourses on "magick" and "Druidism" until the recent completion of *Grade-III* as "Mardukite Systemology." Between these *Grades*, a *Seeker* discovers abundant source material known as the "Mardukite Core" comprising *Grade-II*. These *Grades* also loosely follow a premise for organization set out in the 1990's for *Grade-I* Alumni of "Merlyn Stone's School of Magick"[*] that is referred to elsewhere as "The Sacred Order of the Crystal Dawn." The outline for this premise in 1999 proposed the structuring of "A New Illuminati" using the work published by Joshua Free over the next two decades.

---

[*] Also operating 1998-2000 as "The Elven Fellowship Circle of Magick" in Denver.

There are no strictly enforced "title-badges" and/or "initiations" defining *Grades* when applied to individual *Mardukite Groups* (outside the religious organizational function of *Mardukite Zuism* specifically) for "study" or "instructive" purposes. A *Master* may choose to adopt a particular regimen for their *Seekers* as applicable to each *Grade* and in alignment with the theme and goals of the group. Starting with the original *Grade-I* "Merlyn Stone" volume by Joshua Free—THE SORCERER'S HANDBOOK—reissued for its 21st Anniversary as a collector's edition hardcover, sufficient material is now available in each "core" toward defining group structure as it pertains to the greater "*whole*" at each *Grade*.

Parameters assigned to formal progressive *Grades* are approximately equivalent to the *first three* "*degrees*" of the "Crystal Dawn" program; which is the extent an individual "Chapter" or "Lodge" is allowed to administer (apart from authority of a "Grand Lodge"). For two decades, this clause permitted a *Master* of the *Third Degree* to launch a "Chapter" or "Group" as an official extension of the organization; so long as the *Seeker* had completed the *Master Course*. However, no such *Grade-III* materials were sufficiently supplied as a "core" until 2019 to make this possible.

The basic pattern of development across the *Grades* follows progressive and cumulative ascent up the "Ladder of Lights" or "Gateways to Infinity" first described by the Ancient Mystery School of Mesopotamia as a sevenfold "Babylonian Stargate" system. The chronology of the *Grades* begins with the most apparent and recent influences of the contemporary "New Age"; meaning the modern communication and conception of "magick" and metaphysics—otherwise known as the Western Magical Tradition, which maintained its popularity for the past several thousand years in Europe. This is the essence of *Grade-I*, which is essentially the "*Lunar Gate.*"

A *Seeker* exploring origins behind magickal correspondences, practices, ceremonies and ritualism of various European developments—including everything from ancient Celtic Druids to more modern esoteric Hermetic Orders—will at one juncture or another intersect with the even older Ancient Mystery School present in Mesopotamia —systematized in "Mardukite Babylon" at the inception of the *Age of Aries* (c. 2160 B.C.)—an extension of the former loosely organized Sumerian civilization, now collectively making up *Grade-II* and the key to open the "*Nabu Gate.*"

When a *Seeker* considers this logical progression: we begin with what is most readily familiar and accessible at *Grade-I*, loading the shot in the sling, and then pulling back to the extent that we may be certain, by examining the oldest literary records in *Grade-II*; the very basis for which our *Grade-I* material is actually based, albeit forgotten to the sands of time coupled with thousands of years of programming and encoding separating the two. History and tradition begins with "writing," and so we cannot be certain of anything further than what we have actual accounts of; yet still we find that these *Arcane Tablets* provide an understanding that is milestones beyond what is demonstrated in contemporary society today.

There are many ways of which we can demonstrate how the knowledge between these two *Grades* is bridged and overlaps in application and study; but the *Grades* are distinguished as they are for good reason—and we are not to muddy the waters of a *Seeker's* thinking by incorporating unnecessary complications to instruction. A line has been drawn, if only even from necessity, between the *Grades* by using the *Mardukite Chamberlains Grade-II* material as a benchmark for our evaluation of other materials.

Essentially—all volumes by Joshua Free pertaining exclusively to ancient Mesopotamia are considered *Grade-II*; all volumes pertaining to general mysticism, magick, esoterica, Druidism, &tc are considered *Grade-I*. This is not to say that "higher realizations" are inaccessible from lower *Grade* materials, nor is there a guarantee that "higher realizations" are gleaned directly from reading higher *Grade* materials. A *Seeker* working through the entirety of the first two *Grades* may reach all necessary "ledges" of "knowing" on their own merit, independent of outside instruction. But given that only one-way communication relay takes place from this book-learning, there is no guarantee that an individual will correctly gauge the distance between "ledges" of "knowing" on their ascent up as they leap about unaided.

An early premise of "higher" *Grades* comprised an ORIGINAL THESIS for a new flavor of "New Thought" provided exclusively to *Grade-II* Mardukite Alumni in 2011 as "NexGen Systemology." The official "Core" of *Grade-III* was not released to the public by Joshua Free until late 2019 as "Mardukite Systemology." It is from the vantage point of *Grade-III*, and a mastery of that same tier of knowledge, that we actually treat all of which the *Mardukite Master Course* represents. Although a *Seeker* could certainly remain at one or another *Grade*, an individual must demonstrate total understanding of all three *Grades* to be officially considered a *Master*.

Earliest contributions toward this *Course* from the 1990's are considered *Grade-I*, pertaining to practical magick, general metaphysics, the Western Magical Tradition and its archetypal scions, the *Druids*. The original *Grade-I* volumes pertaining to magick and metaphysics are THE SORCERER'S HANDBOOK and ARCANUM by Joshua Free. In addition to THE DRUID'S HANDBOOK, there are two volumes that both complete the *Druid Cycle* and effectively "bridge" to *Grade-II* elements that incorporate Mesopotamia: DRACONOMICON and ELVENOMICON.[*]

A *Seeker* working through the original *Grade-I* "*Handbooks*" may also choose to take an alternate "bridge" between the ritualism and ceremonialism of *Grade-I* with *Grade-II*, as des-

---

[*] *"Elvenomicon"* formerly released as *"Book of Elven-Faerie"* (from 2004 to 2018) by Joshua Free.

cribed in THE VAMPYRE'S HANDBOOK by Joshua Free.* The original 2015 release of these materials for *Moroii ad Vitam Paramus* served as a contemporary "holding point" for Alumni after the completion of *Grade-II* work, while a "Core" for *Grade-III* developed behind-the-scenes until late 2019. For our purposes, this now means that there are several "entry" points for a *Seeker* to experience glamour and enchantment of the *Grade-I* "*Lunar Gate*" on the way to higher avenues of *Self-Actualization*—which is the ultimate goal behind the *Master* level.

In 2008, existing ARCANUM and ELVENOMICON materials contributed to the establishment of *Mardukite Ministries*, an underground umbrella organization that took control of the former "Merlyn Stone" legacy of Joshua Free as a "ledge" for developing *Grade-II*. By 2009, the *Mardukite Chamberlains* emerged—a global network contributing to progressive generation and dissemination of a "Mardukite Core" of materials, providing the inception of the modern "Mardukite" (and "Mardukite Zuism") paradigms. This living spiritual philosophy dispensed at *Grade-II* is drawn heavily from the ancient cuneiform tablet records of Mesopotamia/Babylon.

Mardukite Chamberlains participated in developing the bulk of material for *Grade-II* from 2009 through 2011. These materials were simultaneously presented in two guises—the *same* materials, but dispensed in two different formats: one emphasizing the *Anunnaki Legacy* as a demonstration of more "academic" and "intellectual" pursuits into ancient history and its esoteric traditions; the other, emphasizing the title of the NECRONOMICON due to the high correlation and association of "New Age" data regarding the ancient "Mardukite Babylonian" tradition. When treated in its entirety as the *Complete Anunnaki Legacy* from within the Mardukite paradigm, presentation of the two "formats" is essentially identical. *Grade-II* should not, however, be confu-

---

* *"The Vampyre's Handbook"* formerly released as *"Vampyre Magick"* by Joshua Free; an anthology edition containing *"Vampyre Bible"* and *"Cybernomicon."*

sed with *any* other outside treatment of the *"Necronomicon"* subject.

Starting in 2009, the original source book of *Grade-II* developed into an anthology composed from individual discourses produced for the *Mardukite Chamberlains* and compiled into NECRONOMICON: THE ANUNNAKI BIBLE. Then, over the next two years, several key elements were added to expand the source book; additionally, several volumes were added to the *Grade-II* core, including Joshua Free's GATES OF THE NECRONOMICON and NECRONOMICON: THE ANUNNAKI GRIMOIRE.‡ These anthologies contain several stand-alone discourses in themselves—all of which were consolidated into a complete *Grade-II* mega-anthology titled NECRONOMICON: THE COMPLETE ANUNNAKI LEGACY (with a special *10th Anniversary Master Edition* released in early 2020).

The gradation (*Grades*) structure and concept of the *Mardukite Master Course* was announced in August 2019 at THE TABLETS OF DESTINY lectures, as described (from transcripts) in the *Grade-III* text of the same title:—

> "Some of you that have been really following along through the materials over the years already have an understanding, from the *Grades* previously provided… And this is one of the keys or secrets held by the *Master*—an individual who has a complete workable understanding of these various levels and degrees represented in former instruction, but they are not themselves formally attached to any of it—drawing up only those solid examples suitable for citation, example and demonstration. So, that's what a Master is, and we are referring now to this intermediary *Grade-III* 'Mardukite Systemology' material as the *Master*

---

‡ *"Gates of the Necronomicon"* anthology includes *"The Sumerian Legacy"* and *"Necronomicon Revelations -or- Crossing to the Abyss"*; *"Necronomicon Grimoire"* anthology includes "*The Complete Book of Marduk by Nabu"* and *"The Maqlu Ritual Book."*

Grade. I expect to also develop a formal instruction course for that, which will solidify the unification of the extant 'Mardukite Core' and NexGen Systemology for this Grade."—*Joshua Free*

The other significant portion of *Grade-III* material is found within the textbook for the CRYSTAL CLEAR Mardukite Systemology Self-Defragmentation Course Program developed by Joshua Free and officially released in December 2019, so as to make certain that proper introductory tools were available for the 2020's decade to usher in a *NexGen* evolution in consciousness. *Grade-III* emphasizes strengthening personal certainty and management of "Reality," employing spiritual philosophies of "Mardukite Systemology." This is our launch point for all further upper-level *Grades*, just as much as it is a capstone representing minimum requirements for our *Mardukite Master Course*—intended to treat <u>all</u> material of *Grades I, II* and *III*.

MATERIALS OF THE
MARDUKITE MASTER COURSE

Since 2009, materials comprising the *Mardukite Research Library* have included all officially published works by Joshua Free to date. From 2008 through 2018, management and responsibility of these materials fell upon the *Mardukite Truth Seeker Press* governed by *Mardukite Ministries* and maintained by the *Mardukite Chamberlains*. As of 2018, a consistent transfer of official responsibility for all materials is increasingly assumed by the *Joshua Free Publishing Imprint*.

Throughout the years, a continuous development ensued, contributing to the release of many materials—including both those mentioned previously in this introduction, and other supplemental works that have appeared or are reissued for posterity. As the work progressed, goals for refinement and consolidation of the knowledge were repeatedly observed in newer editions and publications. Up until recently, the work was exceptionally "fluid" and required considerable attention over the course of its development. Information and discourses were released as they were discovered or refined for many years before appearing as the newly revised "collected works" anthologies and other "collector's editions" in the past year—making the materials more accessible and comprehensible than ever before possible. Goal attained.

It is of benefit for the *Seeker* (and *Master-in-Training*) to see an outright listing of all available graded materials (and their supplements) considered for inclusion as the *Mardukite Master Course*. Titles given represent the most current editions at the time of preparing this introduction. Some *Seekers* may already be in possession of former editions of these materials; and while the titles may change—and volumes may be collected for various anthologies—any *"Liber"*[*] designations used to catalogue the *Mardukite Resear-*

---

[*] The term *Liber* (meaning *book*) is used by esoteric organizations to

ch Library remain fixed to a particular discourse or release in perpetuity. This means, regardless of whatever "title" may be attached to, for example, *Liber-50* (or whatever anthology it may appear in), the material designated "*Liber-50*" is always *Liber-50*, in any of its formats or revisions. Although some *Seekers* have not taken note of these *liber designations*, this internal consistency has been maintained openly and publicly for over a decade.

---

title their work.

MARDUKITE MASTER COURSE TRAINING SCHEDULE

|| GRADE-I || ROUTE OF MAGICK & METAPHYSICS ||

Primary Textbooks:[∞]
>THE SORCERER'S HANDBOOK
>ARCANUM: GREAT MAGICAL ARACNUM

Supplementary:
Additional: *Route of Druidism & The Dragon Legacy*

|| GRADE-I || ROUTE OF DRUIDISM & THE DRAGON LEGACY ||

Primary Textbooks:[*]
>THE DRUID'S HANDBOOK (*Liber-D Series*)
>ELVENOMICON (*Liber-D Series*)
>DRACONOMICON (*Liber-D Series*)

Supplementary:
>THE VAMPYRE'S HANDBOOK
>--The Vampyre's Bible (*Liber V*)
>--Cybernomicon (*Liber V2*)

Optional: *Draconomicon Vol.2: The Pheryllt Researches*
Additional: *Route of Mesopotamian Mysteries*

|| GRADE-II || ROUTE OF MESOPOTAMIAN MYSTERIES ||

Primary Textbooks:[‡]
>NECRONOMICON: THE ANUNNAKI BIBLE
> (-or- THE COMPLETE ANUNNAKI BIBLE)
>--Mardukite Tablet Catalogue (*Liber-N,L,G,9*)
>--The Book of Sajaha-the-Seer (*Liber-S*)
>GATES OF THE NECRONOMICON
>--Sumerian Religion (*Liber-50*)
>--Babylonian Myth & Magic (*Liber-51+E*)

[∞] Grade-I, Route-A Anthology also available—*"The Great Magickal Arcanum"* (2020 Hardcover) by Joshua Free.

[*] Grade-I, Route-D Anthology also available—*"Merlyn's Complete Book of Druidism"* (Hardcover) by Joshua Free.

[‡] Grade-II Anthology also available—*"Necronomicon: The Complete Anunnaki Legacy"* (Hardcover) by Joshua Free.

--Necronomicon Revelations (*Liber-R*)
--Crossing to the Abyss (*Liber-555*)
NECRONOMICON: ANUNNAKI GRIMOIRE
 (-or- PRACTICAL BABYLONIAN MAGIC)
--Babylonian Magic (*Liber-E*)
--The Book of Marduk by Nabu (*Liber-W*)
--The Maqlu Ritual Book (*Liber-M*)
--Enochian Magician's Handbook (*Liber-K*)
Supplementary: Optnl: *The Anunnaki Tarot (Liber-T)*
Addnl: *Route of Mardukite Systemology*

|| GRADE-III || ROUTE OF MARDUKITE SYSTEMOLOGY ||

Primary Textbooks:[∞]
 THE TABLETS OF DESTINY (*Liber-One*)
 CRYSTAL CLEAR (*Liber-2B*)
Supplementary:
 SYSTEMOLOGY: ORIGINAL THESIS (*Liber-S-1X*)
 THE POWER OF ZU (*Liber-S-1Z*)
Optional: *Pantheisticon (300th Anniversary Edition)*
Additional: *Route of The Mardukite Master Course*
 Route of Professional Piloting (Grade-IV+)

[∞] Grade-III Anthology also available—*"The Systemology Handbook"* (Hardcover) by Joshua Free.

INTRODUCING GRADE-I ROUTE-A MATERIALS

Greetings fellow Truth Seekers!

Welcome to the *Mardukite Master Course* for the *Grade-I "A-Cycle"* materials!

When first starting up the *Grade-I* work—which is the first steps plotted toward a higher knowingness of *Life, the Universe and Everything*—the *Mardukite Master Course* issues two potential routes; which are greatly complimentary and not especially exclusive to each other. We will be treating the "A-Cycle" in this unit of the *Course*. Another unit of *Grade-I* work is also available the "*Route of Druidism and the Dragon Legacy*" (otherwise known as the "D-Cycle").

Mardukite Master Course work for the *Grade-I ("A"-Cycle)"Route of Magick and Mysticism"* starts, of course, with a lot of reading—the "*Liber-A Cycle*"—and, if you are so inclined, a significant amount of cross-reference study, "ritual practice" and "metaphysical thought experiments" —all of which are intended to lead a *Seeker* to higher personal realizations (discussed in higher graded work). The purpose of this course *does not* include suspending attentions of a Seeker into lifelong pursuits regarding conventional "magick" or to perpetually the remain the "effect" of an other-determined source of mystical "cause."

As such, subjects of *magick* and the *occult* are treated differently in the *Mardukite Master Course*—and by *Mardukite Masters (Grade-III)*—than what is found anywhere else in metaphysical lore or mystical traditions for nearly 6,000 years...

But...where to begin?

Unlike *Grade-II*, where a *Seeker* may be unwaveringly directed to the original core source book—NECRONOMICON: THE ANUNNAKI BIBLE—as a most logical place to start, the

Grade-I materials have not previously been so clearly structured, leaving many students to meander through the bulk of THE GREAT MAGICKAL ARCANUM in attempts to gain a working knowledge of the Western Magical Tradition—yet a true understanding of the great "unspeakable arcanum" comes from a comprehension of what *is not* being said directly within its pages of collected records and esoteric lore, but is instead suggested by the sum-all of what *is* presented.

To provide a clearer structure for successful study: October 2020, the entire *Liber-A Cycle* of GREAT MAGICKAL ARCANUM is available in a single Master Edition volume that includes the complete text of the SORCERER'S HANDBOOK OF MERLYN STONE as an introduction, and is supplemented by THE LOST BOOKS OF MERLYN STONE for its respective *Grade-I Mardukite Master Course*.

Arrival of THE GREAT MAGICKAL ARCANUM "Master Edition" puts an entire Esoteric Research Library of the *Grade-I —Route of Magick and Mysticism* accessibly at a *Seeker's* fingertips in one single volume, collected writings by Joshua Free spanning nearly a quarter-of-a-century—since the original underground release of SORCERER'S HANDBOOK in 1998. Prior to inclusion of the supportive material, some *Seeker's* found approaching a mighty tome like THE GREAT MAGICKAL ARCANUM for their core instruction somewhat intimidating when not treated systematically. A basic sequence of study for the *Grade-I "Route of Magick"* appears in the Master Edition as follows:

1. SORCERER'S HANDBOOK (*"Introduction"*)
2. ARCANUM (*"The Great Magical Arcanum"*)
3. THE LOST BOOKS OF MERLYN STONE

To further bridge developments of *Grade-I* into *Grade-II* and *Grade-III*, additional training supplements may be found in a separate volume—*Liber-V*—THE VAMPYRE'S HANDBOOK by Joshua Free. An anthology concerning the *"Route of Druidism" Grade-I* material is also available separately as

MERLYN'S COMPLETE BOOK OF DRUIDISM. Naturally, the ultimate goal of the *Mardukite Master Course* is to reach a completion of *Grade-III* work; thus the material within *Grade-I* should be examined and experimented freely, but with those "higher" ends in mind—always.

The introductory text—SORCERER'S HANDBOOK—is a basic primer of magickal fundamentals, introducing key concepts and ideas developed for a "magickal" paradigm. These remain a relevant and effective sequence of study—just as they were in the 1990's—but which may now be further enhanced with "cross-reference research" within THE GREAT MAGICKAL ARCANUM—which forms the main body of the "Cycle-A" (*Arcanum*) anthology. Once you have familiarized yourself with the basic premise of Magick, then proceed with a full study of the ARCANUM material—which a *Seeker* will discover is actually a composite collection of various subjects arranged "A-to-Z" and of which may be cross-referenced using bold-faced words as "links" to other related sections.

There are many common points that bridge *Grade-I* materials for the *Route of Magick and Mysticism* with further *Grade-II* material pertaining to Mesopotamia, Mardukite Babylonia and the Anunnaki paradigm. This is increasingly evident as a *Seeker* works successively through THE GREAT MAGICKAL ARCANUM and is able to glean the deeply hidden links to an original and archetypal Mystery School born in the Ancient Near East and expanding its integration globally.

The core of *Grade-I* material is meant to prepare "higher reaching" Seekers with the information kept in "New Age" libraries, but it is not the final end point of our *Master Course*. The ARCANUM tome is meant only to reveal an entry-point that many spend their remaining lives working out to discover. The author has done that work for you—so you need not be the effect of it or make the purpose of existence to uncover it. Now *you have it*—and higher *Grades* are more easily reachable!

: LECTURE 1—COURSE INTRODUCTION :
(September 21, 2020)

Greetings and welcome to the Mardukite Academy! And it is this, the 21st of September 2020—which is the Autumn Equinox. Of course, that is not why I've called you here today. As you remember, the notice said: *"Class is in session!"* So—what does that mean?

Well, I'm very pleased to announce the completion of the Master Edition volumes that comprise this *Mardukite Master Course*. This has been a long time coming and expected and with the completion and release of *The Great Magickal Arcanum*, we are well on our way now. So, I'm here to deliver something very special—which is the *Mardukite Master Course*.

The purpose of this really—not only for the *Mardukite Academy* and the *Systemology Society*, which the course serves—is to provide "master instruction" for "Masters." And by that, I mean "instructors." And this is important, because unfortunately, as a writer—someone who has a tendency sometimes to sit back up into the "Ivory Tower" and kind of "look out" and deliver the course materials and get feedback along the way—*twenty-five* years has gone into this. And I've never delivered candid personal instruction of the (full) material.

Now, some of you here have obviously been to previous courses and demonstrations, workshops, and what we are doing now is to be certain of the duplication of the material and the knowledge; for me to bring this to you in a very chronological and systematic presentation, for the purposes of duplication; and to ensure, certify and provide professional qualifications for mastering these materials—as it says on the sheets, that's the purpose of this course.

The purpose of this course—this is not a dictation. We are recording this for posterity and to deliver an accurate "Master Course" hereafter. So, I'm doing this *once!* Doing it once and providing it to you, hoping we go out and present this masterful collection of material that we call the "Master Grades"—the "master work" and, of course, now a "Master Course."

So, what is this? It *is* a "course." I'm not going to sit up here and *read* to you the materials. It's important that you *have* access to these materials—whether it's the Master Editions we have here, or however else that you've been able to collect the material over the years. Not much has changed concerning the material; only the *presentation*, and for the purposes of this course and what we are doing now, the *gradation* of it: having "grades"—"grades" and "routes" of *knowledge.*

This Master Course is intended to deliver these Grades and Routes of knowledge in a way that an artist *masters* their craft; and that is what we mean by *mastery.* And there are three Master Grades. Of course, in the Systemology Society, we are working now on Grades IV (*four*) and V (*five*)—and that's important, because that lets you know we are moving somewhere; that there is somewhere to go. But we've also capped this off, in terms of the "Master" work and the "Master Grades" and that (was) completed with the 2019 release of *Crystal Clear.*

What we have now is a graded, structured, method of relaying knowledge that is essentially the result of my own research and discovery using esoteric technologies of the mind and spirit for the past twenty-five years. So, it's high time here with my Silver Anniversary—going now twenty-five years from 1995 to 2020 now; so, I capped off the Master Course and the Master Grades with three levels—three "grades"—which composes four "routes."

Although many people will be able to access a wide amount of knowledge from the Master Course (lectures) specifically and exclusively, this is an appendix and supplement to the literary work that is more widely available: the books. And my original intent in doing this was actually only to deliver the Master Course to those that had actually worked through the first three grades of material on their own. For example, those present here today in this room have all done so. And that's a benefit to us *here*, but for those listening to the recordings later on: again, the purpose of this is to solidify the work through these three grades.

By the "three grades" I mean basically everything that I have written and released between 1995 and 2019—it all relates to a singular stream of instruction. It's now been able to be divided, classified and collected: we have these anthologies, each which represent a different "route." I'll get into the grades and routes in a minute: but it's important, even though we are beginning at the *beginning* and some people may only be interested in accessing certain aspects and properties of the grand scheme of this—this *Pathway*—I want to take this first introductory lecture and just *introduce* the course and give you a bit of a reality on what we are going to be handling on the total scope of this work.

[...] Three grades which pertain to a chronology of time. We're dealing with first what's most accessible. We're going to deal with the esoteric and the occult semantics and the New Age revivals and traditions that have sprung up in America and mainly imported from Europe—and primarily Western Europe at that. And that history. And that's "Grade-I" (*one*) and we call that the "Western Magical Tradition." You are probably *most* familiar with the semantics of the Western Magical Tradition whenever you're dealing with popular "New Age" traditions and revivals: the *Wiccan* and *witchcraft* traditions probably being the most prominent with pop-culture. Even "*vampyrism*" falls into that.

You're seeing a lot of sub-culture, "dark" concepts, mystical concepts, (all) becoming more (main)-stream again—as they were once before with "fantasy" literature. I mean, we have *Harry Potter* now, and *Lord of the Rings*... a lot of mysticism making a return into modern consciousness and a lot of this drawn from elements that have been revived in, what we call, the "Western Magical Tradition." And the figures of the past—of course, people are familiar with Aleister Crowley, and some of these others that have made bigger names for themselves: they all represent that. And that's Grade-I (*one*). And for that we can consider everything in the present, for example, the last one-hundred years or so of the "magical revival" extending back through medieval Europe and, of course, back into the time of the ancient Druids and the shamanic practices that were conducted all throughout that territory, which have become now, a part of mythology and folklore.

Now Grade-I (*one*) is unique in the fact that we've actually divided it into two routes. There is one route which is obviously a broad introduction to the Western Magical Tradition, like what I've described—and then the development of it specifically in Europe, the structure of that and its systematization in Celtic Druidism (or even just "Druidism," not even specific to what we allocate as the Celtic lands of Britain and Ireland and so forth). So, that's Grade-I (*one*).

In Grade-II (*two*), we have what we call the "Ancient Mystery School of Mesopotamia." And that's actually an element that is pretty paramount to our tradition here and structure of learning and what we named ourselves "Mardukite" after. All that goes back to Mesopotamia and Grade-II (*two*).

There's a lot of overlapping between the routes: for example, "Route-A" named after *Arcanum* and also a point of "beginning."

The *Arcanum* volume—"Route-A" which is a very broad approach. And then "Route-D" named for "Druidism"—and, of course, elements of the two routes overlap.

And when you start to stretch back farther beyond even Druidism, we reach, what we consider the origins of the Western Magical Tradition: as we can demonstrate it in the expansion of culture, the literary traditions that have been passed down, the iconic themes, emphasis on the dragon and certain mythological themes that have been duplicated through various cultures, and which are actually more widely known—as opposed to Mesopotamia, which has actually remained in the far depths and reaches of human consciousness, and what we consider the origins of human civilization in terms of its systematization and the actual social and civic programming and the manner which we have been operating for thousands of years. And we treat that in Grade-II (*two*).

Now, we've gone from what's accessible then, to farther reaches into the past—to about the extent that we can go in terms of literary records. In Grade-III (*three*), what we are working with is a composite of all of it, because: these (grades) are not exclusive to one another, however, our understanding of them becomes more and more refined. Because what we've actually found is that: since the time of ancient Mesopotamia and the origins of a lot of these systems, various cultures and the passage of time and relay of communication *not being perfectly duplicated*, it has caused a *degradation*... we keep moving down *from* what *was* once a perfected state or more perfected knowledge, not closer *to* one.

So, rather than do what many have done—and this is something that has been very common with those that work with what we now only classify as Grade-I (*one*) materials and treat those as a whole. A lot of people reach the vista of Grade-I (*one*), which is represented equally by the *lunar level* or the *Sphere of the Moon* or *veil*, or however you want to classify that—and that's figurative only. But it all does seem to work out that way: in terms of the planetary alignment to these grades; and most of you are familiar with the classification from the "*Ladder of Lights*" within the Mesopotamian tradition. And that's what our grades are actually based on.

So, in (Grade) *one*, *two* and *three*: we are dealing with *the Moon*, we are dealing with *Mercury* and we are dealing with *Venus*. And in the Mesopotamian tradition: that would be *Nanna* (*Sin*), *Nabu* and *Ishtar* (*Inanna*). And at Grade-III (*three*) we are dealing with material of the *Ishtar Gate* or the "third veil" of the true ascent up the "*Ladder of Lights*" or "*Pathway to Self-Honesty*" or what we are also referring to as "*Gateways to Infinity*" in (upper-level) Systemology.

When you put all these together, we are trying to take it to a *higher* level and not simply remain fixed at this "occult," "ritual magic" or "ceremonial" or even "mythological" framework. And we are moving forward in Grade-III (*three*) with a "futurist" or "NexGen" methodology, which we are calling "Mardukite Systemology."

"Mardukite Systemology" as Grade-III (*three*)—and being an encompassing pinnacle of what we are working at for the "Master Course"—is really the perspective that an "instructor" or "Master" of this material is approaching this whole body of material with. And that is why I say, I'm not trying to duplicate lectures or recordings of the actual (written) material itself, because we are approaching it with—at least for the purposes of this course—a Grade-III (*three*) understanding.

This is not to say that you will have had to work through all the materials already in order to understand this (course). However, we aren't treating, for example, the "route of magick and mysticism," and (route of) "druidism" and even ancient Mardukite Mesopotamia, as fixed encompassed "wholes" of which there is nothing outside of. Because, unfortunately that's what happens with most paradigms.

A paradigm becomes a continuous whole in which everything operates and works fine so long as you stay within it—as soon as you step out of it, well, that's where things break apart. And so we are not confining ourselves to that.

This is important for me to point out because this is actually what separates the average "initiate" or "esoteric practitioner" and so forth, from what we are treating as a "Master." Because at Grade-I (*one*)—I'll be honest with you—many of the people I have encountered in my journeys rarely get beyond that as an *actualization point.*

And so when we refer to the "seven levels" or "Seven Gates" or "seven steps" up to *Infinity*, the thing that's been discovered from a Master level understanding is that this structure of veils and thresholds that we cast off as we move upward is actually mirrored at each level.

Most practitioners that break through the Earth Gate—they finally realize they are not these physical bodies, there is something more—they break into this first veil of the *Moon* and *enchantment* and the glamours of mysticism, the lights and rainbow before them, and that there is this whole other world. There is a sense of arrival. There is a sense of having a change of Beingness—in being at one point as opposed to a previous point. And in that, there is usually a sense of completion—that a cycle has been completed, that there has been a breakthrough, that a threshold has been passed.

And many people will then work through the Seven Veils *within* the confines of that first grade, that first level—and each time feeling more and more of that accomplishment, more and more of that (feeling of) arrival. What ends up happening with that mentality, is that it usually strengthens and solidifies the [first grade] as a whole, as an encompassed whole.

For example: Grade-I (*one*)—or either of the routes of Grade-

I (*one*)—could be treated as a complete wholeness or continuity; they function as a paradigm; they are functional. They have a series of principles; a series of concepts, axioms; symbols that represent various ideals—and when you put them together, they seem to have a causal relationship, which when using only that paradigm, can be defined with that paradigm.

This is not much different that what we do with the *physical* "Earth Gate" scenario on the planet Earth, with, for example, the "physical sciences." We can usually take a look with physical instruments and we examine, as an observer, the consequences or the causal actions of various sequences. And we define those consequences based on that paradigm. And we say, "Well, if we do this, this happens," or "this takes place" and so-and-so... and *it works!* It *seems* to work. It only breaks down when you step outside the paradigm.

What we are working towards is really a *"paradigm-free"*-paradigm—one where we are not restricted to the semantics of one set of mythologies or cultural symbols or another; or even have to spend a lot of time—which we do in certain respects just to break it down for you—spend a lot of time in trying to make all of the comparisons that are possible. Well, you know "*Zeus*" is also "*Jupiter*," which is also "*Marduk*" and then if you compare *this* mythology here of an underworld with the "descent" over *here*... and so forth... you could spend an entire lifetime with that.

And it *is* a lot of interesting stuff—there's a lot of interesting facts and data that you could do with that. And *we* cover that. That's one of the things, for example, *The Great Magickal Arcanum* and the discoveries made in the Mesopotamian tradition, where we find the root or archetypes of these mythological, for example, "gods" and "goddesses" or certain epics or stories or themes, which later, other cultures kind of "copy-and-pasted" in their own way. But *never* a true *duplication*.

So we have all these various languages and names and so forth, depending on where cultures were located.

For example, a culture that existed in more desert terrain would seem to place more emphasis on *water* and the "Waters of Life" and deities associated with *water* and *fertility* in that respect in order to survive. Whereas, in the northern countries, you see more of an emphasis on *fire*, because that was what they used more prominently as their means of material survival and to keep warm. And then of course you see veneration—the old "pagan" veneration—of these elements, which were used for survival. At that perspective and within those paradigms it seemed to make sense.

Structuring your agricultural—the rise and fall of tides and the seasons—and structuring the observance of different times of year with the planting of the crops and so forth; well this was very paramount to the survival of the ancient pagan man and society.

So, what I have done: we have a series of materials to go through in order to accomplish this (course). It is a large understanding of background to bring, what I am hoping to deliver (here) as "Mardukite Systemology," which is basically and essentially a higher understanding of the (Master) work and what we can do with this to further ourselves and get out of these trappings that have been laid down. Because each of these veils—we are not *adding*; that is another one of the illusions of this work.

We are not *adding* the actual *layers* to us as we move through this; we are *taking layers away*—aspects that have actually been artificially implanted or taken on or enshrouded us, to bring us down to this Earth Gate, to bring us down to this perspective where the Human Condition is basically fixed to believe that "it is in-and-of these bodies." And now most of you here today—and those listening [reading]—most of you know that there is *something more*, otherwise you wouldn't even be here and you wouldn't be listening.

You really can't convince people of this type of work. It's something that has to be realized and actualized on an individual basis—or it won't be *real*. It won't be real for *you*; it won't be real for *them* (or that guy over there). To share a reality on this is to basically deliver a duplication of what I am presenting in the "Mardukite Master Course."

This is a professional course. Our intention is, of course, to certify instructors to be able to deliver this information on a local basis. And to do that—to maintain the professionalism of the "Mardukite" name, the "Mardukite Academy" and the "Systemology Society." It's important that we deliver this and have it down and have it recorded so that it can be delivered a concise and systematic way.

This course is essentially chronological—of my own personal journey. Though, that just so happens to be the way it worked out. Not necessarily what was meant to be, but my introduction in the mid-90's was with traditional ritual magick and ceremonial magic. And my initiation to Druidism. And that was kind of my own Grade-I (*one*) crash-course.

My intentions (were) in understanding the roots of what I was "learning" and the roots of what other people seemed to be *really* latched onto in the mid-90's and the late 90's when occultism and pagan revivals and witchcraft and Druidism and a lot of this was making a serious resurgence... as it had done several generations prior, with the foundations—the "Hermetic Order of the Golden Dawn" and "Argentium Astrum" and "Aurum Solis" and all kinds of "Rosicrucian" and "Theosophical" groups.

So, we are coming up again on a new era... and what is this leading to? We haven't seen a great improvement on the planet—in terms of society, civilization, where the material technologies have brought us—so, we need "*Masters.*" We need people who are able to grasp this material and deliver it, because it *is* a "higher" understanding. And it *does* follow a premise that I originally set down back in the 90's.

It's taken a long time to arrive here, but I'm pleased to announce that it actually has; and I'm excited to deliver what will be essentially the most complete esoteric course, when you factor in the literary materials and what we'll be going through—the most concise course on these subjects. And for the sole purpose of *flattening* these *waves* that we have *collapsed* through the last thousands of years, that have separated us from a higher, truer, point of being and knowing.

And that is the intention. As an upper-level Mardukite Academy Systemology Course, which, all of you are ready for—I'm taking a step back from working on the higher grades to deliver what is going to be a concise step and advancement into what we are now dealing with, with Systemology. And Mardukite Systemology requires a greater control and actualization and mastery of Self than really has ever been truly demonstrated before through these other paradigms—although they have all led to, or believed to have been leading to, these higher points of actualization.

The magicians and wizards and sages and priestesses and so forth of the last several thousand years were all following in the shadows of this higher and truer point of being and knowing, and the understanding of that. But they were doing it within their own cultural ways and within the confines of the language and understanding of those societies. We really have nothing to gain by performing a perfect duplication or reconstruction of *those* traditions, which we've already found the limits of, and now we can grade on this chart and on the *Pathway to Self-Honesty* and beyond.

I'm really looking forward to seeing what this can lead to once more instructors, Masters, individuals—and even those who have no real intention of getting involved in the organization and structure of our work—can create a better world, since we are all participants in that here, and we can really only create to the extent that we can imagine.

: LECTURE 2—INTRODUCING THE MATERIALS :
(September 21, 2020)

I wanted to just kind of fly through the materials—the textbooks—that we'll be using, that we'll be referring to in this course; that you'll be using as Masters and instructors when you're doing this course yourselves, with your own Seekers. And it's ironic that we're doing this now. Two decades ago, actually, I had planned on establishing something like this. I had high aspirations for what we were calling at the time, in the late-1990's, the "Order of the Crystal Dawn."

Within that structured program, I had established that a "Master" of the "Third Degree" would be able to launch a chapter or a group of their own—or a lodge—as an extension of the organization. Of course, there were no "Master" level materials. It's really up until 2019 that were no Grade-III (*three*) to really speak of.

As I mentioned: the pattern of development of the grades works cumulatively up the *Ladder of Lights*, the planetary methodology—the sevenfold Babylonian Stargate system—however you want to look at that. Now, to be completely honest, it does—as I mentioned in the previous lecture—follow my own chronology of publishing. It [the Course and grades] wasn't really intended to work out that way, it just worked out that way.

These materials now fall within the domain of these four textbooks. And these textbooks include materials that you and your Seekers and so forth would potentially already have in other formats. So, it's important that we go through what is actually within these, because you may have them in other versions—and then of course, just to have an overview and a shared reality on what all we are going to be dealing with.

Logically, you are going to be using materials first and foremost with what's most accessible at the Grade-I level, and then working from what that understanding is based on—once you work through Grade-I. You logically do actually arrive at Grade-II, and there are a lot of ways in which that can be worked with, overlapped, and inherently we kind of fixed as like, "Mardukite Zuism" and the "Mardukite" tradition, and so forth—we've kind of fixed our primary entry point at Grade-II.

Within Grade-II and also encompassing Grade-I, it's pretty much the foundation in which people are going to be able to relate to—especially in their own supplemental researches. We're dealing with accessible stuff... to the extent that history and tradition really, for our purposes, begins with "writing." And so, we can't really be certain of anything beyond what we have the actual written accounts of. We can *speculate*. But, what we have dealt with from the Mardukite perspective and the Mardukite Chamberlains (Research Organization) and the Council of Nabu—all of this that's developed over the past decade—more than a decade—we've really emphasized the literary tradition.

The milestone and the pinnacle of our (literary) understanding is really the "Arcane Tablets." And those we find on the ancient cuneiform literature—which we deal with at Grade-II. What mainly pertains to the material that you're going to find most accessible. Our Systemology is a further understanding and development what is relayed verbatim in the traditions and symbolism and methods of the past.

Now, once you understand "Mardukite Systemology"—from a Grade-III perspective—you can actually *see* how the lower-grades function and are effective in their own—within their own—paradigm. That higher understanding... there was an early premise for what's now Grade-III, that I released as *Systemology: The Original Thesis.*

And it provided Mardukite alumni with a "new thought," because that's essentially what Systemology became: an extension as being a "New Thought" movement of the Mardukite Chamberlains; a way of taking what was uncovered with Grade-I and Grade-II research and discovery and bringing it into present time—bringing it into the future—developing something that is far and beyond what these previous paradigms have been able to attain within and as themselves.

That doesn't mean that you have to buy into our Systemology in order to attain new heights and actualization in your existence. However, if you do examine what we are doing with it, and the systematization of it, it really is a universal approach. It doesn't invalidate the lower grades—and that was never the intention. In referring to them as "lower grades" we don't mean necessarily "lesser than" or "subordinate to" in a traditional ethical civic sense.

The "lower grades" are foundations on which we have a greater and higher understanding accessible to us by using the relay of the past thousands of years of information and trying to make sense of it. Which is ironic, because that unification is actually the hidden meaning behind the title *Great Magickal Arcanum.* Now, *The Great Magickal Arcanum*—the Grade-I Route-A textbook—this is where it all begins for us on the Master Course and with instruction. What that is in reference to is really the encompassing of the whole.

What the "Great Magickal Arcanum" is: it is the unspeakable knowing and Beingness that is attained by having a unified understanding of, and a workable and effective knowledge, on which any kind of wisdom can be attained for application. If we look at all these books here—now this can become quite overwhelming—it really begins with the earliest contribution toward this course in the 1990's, which is, it pertains to practical magick, general metaphysics, what I referred to as the Western Magical Tradition.

So, the Grade-I volume... *The Sorcerer's Handbook* was really the first primary work that I had developed for wide-stream distribution. There was a work that I had done previously, the *Draconomicon*, which is also dealt with in Grade-I Route-D, pertaining to the Druids.

The Sorcerer's Handbook and *The Great Magickal Arcanum* comprises the A-Cycle or Route-A of "Magick and Mysticism" for Grade-I. There have been many different editions of *The Sorcerer's Handbook*—more than I can actually count, or have kept track of... I think we're up to the eighth or ninth or tenth now... The 21st Anniversary edition was released in 2019; the first time it was released in hardcover. And it included *The Lost Books of Merlyn (Stone)* and the stuff about the "Crystal Dawn" that I was referring to as a structure.

One of the things I did, given that we were working on Master Course volumes this time around... and I looked at *Arcanum*, and I thought, well, you know we've been compiling all these other books together to make these Master Editions—these large textbook sized [*laughs*] Master Editions—and I looked at *Arcanum* and it was pretty much already that on its own. I thought, well, you know the only other material that really goes with that, which actually provides a structure for it, was the *Sorcerer's Handbook*.

So, this new *Great Magickal Arcanum: A Master Course in Magick for Modern Wizards*, this edition which is technically the 13th Anniversary edition of *Arcanum*, actually includes the text of *The Sorcerer's Handbook* as an "Introduction." So, you have the structure of the *Sorcerer's Handbook* and then you have the complete *Great Magickal Arcanum*.

Although most get wrapped (up) into the mechanics, the systems, the correspondences—all of the magical correspondences—and the planets, the herbs and the incense, and all of that, of Grade-I, there are many high level realizations that are attainable at that point.

And unfortunately most individuals that participate or are initiated into these traditions, they don't usually reach them with that. They usually remain quite enamored with the *lunar level* of enchantments and mysticism and the colorful lights and arrays that are accessible.

As I say, the magical paradigms, you are usually so "excited" about getting "out of" this more mundane material existence, that almost any larger—"larger than" or "greater than"—has to be, you know, "well, *this* is where *it's* at." So most of them end up—they talk about "stepping outside the box" and "thinking outside the box," but most of them step out to get into another box, and that's been mostly established in our systematic way of looking at all these different paradigms.

The Great Magickal Arcanum is a way of trying to treat all of the paradigms in a form of unification; and this is something that again—the average initiate, not looking deeper into the work of the Mardukite Academy or the Master Course or Systemology—in the past, has run the risk of really just looking at *Arcanum* as this "tremendously impressive" A-to-Z "*encyclopedia*" of "magick" and, you know, a "collected works" of all these different "rituals" and "spells" and "traditions" and so forth; and well... unfortunately, that's pretty much where it ends, rather than seeing the greater picture.

Now, there are some articles concerning "metaphysics" and "epistemology" and various philosophies and things in that book, where if you can begin to tie that in with the other traditions, you'll see that's where it was intended to be all along; that we were intending on a unification into a higher systemology.

It should be understood that there is a "systemology" present in the work, underlying this work, from the very beginning. That never changed.

It may have taken a couple decades to really synthesize a published sequence of material, but really we're dealing with the same goals, aspirations and fundamentals toward Ascension, and what we call the *Pathway to Self-Honesty* and *Gates to Infinity* and so forth. We're dealing with the same thing at each grade.

The fundamentals, the purpose—what Life is actually doing here in this universe—these don't change with the paradigms or with each sequence and series of cultural traditions and methodologies. It's simply the flavor that changes; the context; the pictures; the patina; the facade—whatever you want to call it—the different masks. And with those, different attributes, the descriptions, guidelines, boundaries, that we might call "personalities" or even the personalities, not just of an individual, but of the entire culture, which includes their perception of ethics, or you know, as they treat it at lower levels as morals, but basically the religious connotations and the fundamentals behind that—whether or not they are being enforced or being observed properly or being punished, that definitely changes from culture to culture, as do the attitudes, as is the willingness of what is considered acceptable.

We're looking at a higher treatment of this knowledge now—particularly from Grade-III. A Grade-III "Master" can certainly be an instructor for a local branch of the Mardukite Academy and deliver courses on specifically "magick" or "Druidism" or any of these which are specific "routes," specific "courses" and curriculum that can be delivered in exclusion to others. It might be that someone only has an interest in, for example, the "Druidic" and "earth mysteries" and "Elven" and "shamanic" ways that we relay also in Grade-I, in these other materials here: *Merlyn's Complete Book of Druidism*.

The point being that a "Master" of this knowledge—from a "Master Grade" perspective—will be able to deliver it in such a way as to demonstrate higher-level principles of Systemology and our futurist and metahuman pursuits within the lower grade material. As a result, we're not going to leave Seekers meandering about and wandering blind through these catacombs of esoteric mysteries and forbidden knowledge and old forgotten lore or leave them to their own accord that way. That's been done. You take a look at the bookshelves anywhere—the "New Age" sections of a bookstore or the collection in people's library, an individual's library that they might use, and you'll see this: a wide collected composite of knowledge and so on and so forth.

Then you take a look at the individual and where has it gotten them.

Now, some people—don't get me wrong—some people have been able to access some amazing vistas from all this, and that's inherently what these traditions were meant to do from their inception. Whether or not that continued later on, or whether they became further and further methods of entrapment into this material existence; that remains to be seen.

The work itself can be demonstrated at whatever level and grade of materials an individual is willing to—well, essentially take responsibility for knowing, to the point that they can actually grasp this knowledge. In Druidism, when—and this was very controversial when I presented it—so, we've dealt with *Sorcerer's Handbook* and *Arcanum* as *The Great Magickal Arcanum* now for Route-A, so let's talk about Route-D, which is "Druidism" and the "Dragon Tradition."

Route-D is really a composite of *The Druid's Handbook*, *Draconomicon* and the three books that comprise the *Elvenomicon*, which used to be known as the *Book of Elven-Faerie*. We changed it to "Elvenomicon," primarily because *Book of Elven-Faerie* technically was only the title for the first of the three books that that material was previously released as, and so there were other aspects to that. So, now it's *Elvenomicon*.

And those books are all now contained in *Merlyn's Complete Book of Druidism: A Master Course in Druidry for Modern Druids.*

In moving to that material from the material in *Arcanum* or *Sorcerer's Handbook*, we find of course, the primordial, and nearly prehistoric roots of the "earth magic" and natural traditions of Europe. And that's important; that's a pretty integral step between what we've barely been able to uncover now from the "Arcane Tablets" and the "New Age" traditions as we have today; that's basically the Western Magical Tradition. So, now we have "Druidism."

Druidism—this was very controversial when I developed the research for it—I found to really tie back into ancient Mesopotamia as an origin. I mean, I had heard and been taught, well, "Atlantis" and the "Druids" and so on, ...came out of nowhere and walked up from the sea, or however that all happened. But, nobody really knew, and no one really discussed it, and that's something we will delve into further along the course. Because even though I did present a lot of material about it, it's only been recently confirmed within the last couple years.

So a lot of the more controversial aspects of what we're presenting as this wide encompassing "Mardukite Master Course," a lot of that is no longer—well, whether or not it's controversial or not, there's been a lot more validity to its acceptance. At least in terms of things we can put our finger on; things we can demonstrate. This work as a whole is really only effective to the point that it can be demonstrated and, which is of course, communicated, and then of course, also equally effectively understood.

And an individual will really only understand this to the degree that they have reached a realization of as a platform of understanding. And so we have a bridge between *Arcanum* and just the general magical tradition as it's relayed in the contemporary New Age, and then "Druidism."

And there is a direct bridge between "Druidism" and its "Dragon Tradition" and so forth, to Mesopotamia. And then of course, by the time we get to Mesopotamia, we're dealing with what also became a subject of great controversy when I released it under the pretense of "Necronomicon."

And that seemed to be a real good clincher for a lot of people as to whether or not they even recognized or knew of our work; they knew the "Necronomicon" and they knew this had to be something about that and of course, the "Anunnaki" as was firmly expressed in its title. But what that ended up leading to was—in 2009, I established the Mardukite Chamberlains in 2009.

Now, the original Mardukite movement was actually launched with the material of *Arcanum* in combination with the material from what is now the *Elvenomicon*. So, you combine those two together an in 2008, I launched the "Mardukite Ministries," "Mardukite Zuism." The Mardukite Research Organization and the actual Chamberlains and association of involvement developed more strongly in 2009, and that continued—in terms of the development of the "Core" (materials)—that continued pretty strongly through 2011.

And so now we were dealing with what we now consider Grade-II, and it was basically—I would say it was a point when many individuals in this room today—it was the point when some "beacon" went off, or you were able to locate the Mardukite movement, or you knew something of the "Anunnaki" or the "Simon Necronomicon" and discovered that this material (of ours) existed.

So, for all the grief I have received for the treatment of this material as "Necronomicon" for ancient Mesopotamia: it was an "entry-point"—as is "Druidism" an entry-point; as is the "Route of Magick and Mysticism" an entry-point. These are *entry-points* for your Seeker to "enter" the *Pathway to Self-Honesty*. They become limited and fixed (only) when treated as the "end-all be-all" within themselves. But these are all "entry-points" in which to bring someone up into this *Pathway*, which of course leads to "Mardukite Systemology."

It was in 2009 that the work for the source-book of—what is now Grade-II—developed into an anthology in itself. Now, there were several companion texts going with this, expansions of it, translations and so forth; and now we have what is the *Necronomicon: The Complete Anunnaki Legacy*, and this hardcover Master Edition is the primary textbook. There is only one "route" in Grade-II. Grade-I is the only grade that has two "routes."

So there is only one route within Grade-II and it is all encompassing within this *Necronomicon: The Complete Anunnaki Legacy*. And this includes all of the materials that were developed for the "Mardukite Chamberlains" over the course of a decade; which I believe there is literally over a dozen—something like *fifteen*—different discourses and books and releases contained within *The Complete Anunnaki Legacy* here, this edition.

This brings us up to, again, "Mardukite Systemology." And... [*sighs*] ...this, again, this is a new edition. This is a new edition of the course. And although it was the intention at the time—I did release several dispersed lectures, most of which, the materials for that: if you look back, there is the *Systemology: The Original Thesis*, it contains these little booklets that came out a decade ago. It paved the way for "well, we know this is going somewhere, but where is it going"— and it took another decade of work, really, to bring this to some kind of effective understanding and workability. That came about... I not only completed the work for Grade-III independently... there had been no discussions about Systemology in any way shape or form for a while, pretty much, except for some of the "Vampyre" work in 2015.

After 2013, there was very little that was going into Systemology directly on a visible level.

All that work was being conducted underground. So, we basically compiled Grade-III—in terms of publishing—over a period of about three or four months. All that material is now contained in this Master Edition of the *Systemology Handbook*. This contains, well it contains a lot of bonus and additional material than what is contained in the individual volumes itself—but primarily the two fundamental... well, the textbook for Grade-III, which was *The Tablets of Destiny*, and then the practical guide, which was kind of a follow up to the methodology presented in there, which is *Crystal Clear*.

Crystal Clear is also the Mardukite Systemology Self-Defragmentation Course, and that I presented in December 2019, right after in August that year, presenting the *Tablets of Destiny* material and lectures. So, we've been at that... We've been really at that level of work for now about a year, and now with that capped off as Grades *one*, *two* and *three*, we have now what we can deliver as the Mardukite Master Course.

Within that—just in brief—we have the "Route of Magick and Mysticism" in Grade-I, which mainly is the *Sorcerer's Handbook* and *Arcanum*, both of which are now contained in *The Great Magickal Arcanum: A Master Course in Magick for Modern Wizards*. And that's Grade-I Route-A.

Now, Grade-I Route-D, we have the "Route of Druidism and the Dragon Legacy." That pertains to the materials from *The Druid's Handbook*, *Elvenomicon* (the three books composed of the *Book of Elven-Faerie*) and the *Draconomicon*—in addition to some "Pheryllt" research, which is all contained within *Merlyn's Complete Book of Druidism: A Master Course in Druidry for Modern Druids*.

In Grade-II, we have *Necronomicon: The Complete Anunnaki Legacy*. Which includes, within that, all the "Mesopotamian Mysteries" material: the *Anunnaki Bible*, the *Gates* material, *Sumerian Legacy*, the *Necronomicon Revelations*, the *Book of*

Marduk by Nabu, the *Maqlu*, *Babylonian Magic*... all of that... All of that contained in there is Grade-II.

And then finally in Grade-III, released now in this one volume as *The Systemology Handbook*, we have the primary textbooks—*The Tablets of Destiny* and *Crystal Clear*—and then also, within the same Master Edition: the full text of *The Original Thesis* and *The Power of Zu* lectures.

So, within these four Master Edition volumes—3,600 pages worth—within these four volumes you will find all the texts and course material that will be referred to in the Mardukite Master Course.

: LECTURE 3—THE GREAT MAGICAL ARCANUM :
(September 21, 2020)

Alright, so let's go ahead and focus on Grade-I Route-A: The Route of Magick and Mysticism. Now, this is fundamentally the textbook—*The Great Magickal Arcanum*—but when you're leading a Seeker through this part of the Route... you know, originally, *The Sorcerer's Handbook* was compiled specifically for this reason. It was compiled for groups that I was working with back in the mid-90's actually. And it has a pretty concise sequence of development.

If you want to take a Seeker up the *Pathway* of fundamentals as it applies to magic: magickal correspondences, basic techniques and exercises, witchcraft and Wicca, arts of spellcraft and ritual magic, elemental magic and Druid power, the high magick of the Golden Dawn, enochian magick, and then of course, the Necronomicon and Mesopot-

And there, you see, we have a couple bridges. There's a bridge there at the end, of course, with the assumption that an individual might lead directly to Grade-II from the "Route of Magick" using the Necronomicon and Mesopotamia as a bridge. The other being midway there: elemental magic and Druid power being able to tie in to that other route, Route-D, for the grade, because there are many individuals that are going to be more interested in those elements as opposed to the ceremonial magic and high traditions of, for example, the Golden Dawn and enochian practices and so forth.

It should be understood in delivering a course like this to your Seekers, or even as is presented at the Mardukite Academy for this "Magick School," we don't *require* that an individual actually, you know, conduct all these ceremonial ritual practices that are discovered. *The Sorcerer's Handbook* is very concise in its relay and the sequence and moving along someone through the *Pathway* of, at least, occult studies relatively quickly.

The benefit of *Arcanum* as a companion to that, is the ability to pursue deeper explorations as they relate to other explorations and realizations and different paradigms. We really don't want to keep Seekers suspended in lifelong pursuits involving conventional magick—or to keep them perpetually remaining the "effect," as the "magical traditions" tend to do, of some "other-determined" indeterminable source of mystical cause that is *outside* from the individual. The purpose of our tradition is to bring the power and control and command of Self back under the responsibility and management of Self—and not to be looking to outside sources.

Now, what happens is that an individual that looks into, for example, any of the other routes or grades or even Systemology or other pursuits on the internet, or other authors and their literature—they are going to find a lot of this "magical" and "occult" and "mystical" information or semantics being displayed. And that's one of the purposes of the *Great Magickal Arcanum*.

The Great Magickal Arcanum—it took another ten years after the *Sorcerer's Handbook* for me to put together *Arcanum*. And that was release, we used to have, starting with the original one, these "Discovery Events." Now we have conferences, lectures and different things.

On the Summer Solstice 2008, we had "The Great Magical Arcanum Discovery Event" and this was also the "Mardukite Zuism" and "Systemology" founding… technically. We released *Arcanum* to the underground and had an event. We had dozens of people at the event at the original Mardukite Offices. This turned into a series of releases and work under the "Mardukite" banner.

A year later, we had another Discovery Event for the release of *"Liber-N"* as the *"Necronomicon."* Then we would continue each year... annually, we would usually have a big encompassing "this is our year in review" type of event, which was usually solidified with some kind of book or anthology of the work that had taken place during the previous year.

Arcanum is a little different; it's definitely a unique literary contribution of mine, because before all of this other work that I was later known for, or even put together, this synthesized my attempts at that time—in 2008—or what I had done by 2008; it took about two years to actually write out and refine *Arcanum* systematically.

The purpose of it being, not to create a large "A-to-Z encyclopedia of magick" but to actually unify the knowledge that had already come under the folds of the "New Age"—because it was no longer specific to just "magical" and "mythological" forms of occultism; now we were starting to deal with more what was classified as "pseudo-science" or the "meta-psychologies" and even "quantum" and "string-theory." We were seeing the same analysis of "life, universe, everything" taking place around us at, just more varying degrees of external technology and the information age.

We launched the Mardukite movement the same time they turned on the Hadron collider; within the same year—a lot of things taking place now that really weren't there before. Even the semantics of the sciences have been shifting and changing; particularly when you start to deal with "quantum" theories and "string theory."

Now, you don't need to understand those semantics in order to understand what we are dealing with (here); the point being that the work that we're doing and the work that's been relayed, starting with *The Great Magickal Arcanum*, and starting your Seekers right down there with Grade-I, is it's universal.

We're looking at the same objective universe taking place around us, but our understanding of it being fixed to whatever paradigm we are choosing to adopt at the time. My original approach was to simply unify "psychology" and "metaphysics" with the "occult sciences." Now, this is before it was a trendy thing to do. Now you hear all about "quantum fields" and "Akashic realities" and, you know, using "black boxes" and "crystal capacitors" and all kinds of things, but back when we were establishing this, this wasn't even a thing. Just like when we first launched "Mardukite Ministries," the "ancient aliens" wasn't a show on television; "Anunnaki" wasn't a household word or generally known concept.

We were dealing with unfamiliar territory at the beginning of our organization. And there's a lot of things now we might take for granted, but at the time it was "new" and "innovative" and we were still uncertain of where we were exactly putting our next footfall.

With *Arcanum*, there was at least a unifying picture—and the purpose of it: to break down the vocabulary or the semantic barriers that were in place between mythologies, sciences, religions. We weren't seeing—in this information age, and the internet, and all this "freedom of information" that everyone's *pulling for*—that it wasn't necessarily moving us towards a unification—a global unity—or progressing our understanding.

It was an accumulation of more and more facts and this continues to the present day. Without systematically approaching this data, it is virtually impossible to make "heads or tails" out of it; therein lying the "great magical arcanum"—the unintelligibly inarticulate truth behind all this: what it was all pointing towards; what it all means. And that unfortunately when you get down too close into it and too fixed into the little intricacies—as people have a tendency to do—you don't see that picture anymore.

And that seems cliché—oh well, "the closer you look, the less you see." Well, more important than that: "the more fixed the attention is—and the more rigid that its parameters are as to what's possible, acceptable and real—is the defining factor."

So, therein lies, really, the benefit to Route-A; because what magick and mysticism does for most people and what that *lunar level* really is for most people *is* the first breakaway from the heavy pulls and ties that are found—succumbing to and participating and agreeing to only a physical and material form of things.

Obviously we know there is much more. But they become counter-thoughts and counter-productive to our own productivity when we say, "Oh, yes, we know that" but then we go back to the patterns and systematic reactivity of the Human Condition, which only further agrees and validates to the most material mundane levels.

So, we work against ourselves when we just shoot for the stars and try to reach for Infinity and the find that, "well, it's not quite in our grasp," and then we recoil back, and go, "well, I didn't reach it then, so I'm just gonna try a little bit less next time, because really it doesn't seem accessible to me and all of this really seems ridiculous and a bunch of fantasy" and so on and so forth.

Hence, the purpose of our graded system. Because you start to give people—you know, they have these high expectations and goals of what they think different paths or results are going to be for them; and if they don't get those "wins" along the way, they are not going to continue along the way. So, a big part of it is really just understanding what this stuff is. It's not so much important that they practice all these rituals—or experiment with all these spells—and most of this stuff you can really do at a "thought" level.

Although there is a purpose behind making the body do movements at will; making it extend its reach and withdraw; putting significances into objects; and other aspects of ritual—these are all *tools* and that's one of the aspects of the magical tradition that many practitioners really miss out... all of the power and significance and importance gets placed into the *tool* and not the *individual*. You know: the magic is somehow (confined) fixed into the *wand*, and the *wand* is somehow charged independent of the individual and so *that's* where the power lies—again, misplacing "cause" and misplacing the ability to be "source."

That doesn't mean you couldn't in essence—consciously, knowingly and willingly—grant a "Beingness" to a piece of wood with intentions; and because of its particular wood cut at the proper time and season while facing the right direction and standing on one foot... There's no reason why *that* can't be practiced *and* be effective; there's also no reason why *that* is the *only* way things must be practiced *to* be effective and get the results.

We find a rigid constriction that forms when a practitioner believes they have ability but only under the proper conditions and only if the "stars are aligned" and so on and so forth; and this is one of the trappings of the occult. Because it gives the illusion that: "yes there is more than; but it's not *you*"—and you're still putting a misappropriated placement of "source" outside of Self.

You've realized there's something more than the physical universe, so we get to this realm where things are "magical" and things are "enchanting" and it *is* a "more than" or "greater than" but we aren't necessarily free of the Human Condition. We've elevated our Awareness; as we say in Systemology—our "Actualized Awareness." We've elevated our point of Beingness and Knowingness to a point "greater than" or "above" or at a "higher frequency" than what it means to be fixed into the point of view of just, this, "material-meat-body" physical condition.

There is a lot of material out there. And that's one of the things that *Arcanum* is meant to start breaking down. And what it does is it allows—I mean, go off of the *Sorcerer's Handbook* as your basic, you know, here's the steps of actualizing magic. It is effective. It is effective formula and curriculum. It works very expeditiously. But there is obviously a lot more to it.

It was a "handbook" for a reason; that's why it was intended to be a "handbook" as separate from a larger "textbook." It was not meant to replace supplemental studies or other lectures or other lessons, it was simply a "handbook" to have access to the most important aspects of learning the "Route of Magick."

It has been now incorporated into this edition of *The Great Magickal Arcanum: A Master Course in Magick for Modern Wizards*—but as a stand alone, it is an excellent reference in and of itself. Now, *The Great Magickal Arcanum* works in a very systematic way before we're even pushing the concept of "systemology" verbatim. It is intended to be an integral study; it doesn't really have a starting point. And that's why as a stand-alone, either without *The Sorcerer's Handbook* or without some additional background or without being guided a Master in this tradition—the *Arcanum* mainly sits on most people's shelves that have owned it in the last decade, as a reference book. Simply as a reference to look up various topics.

Although it doesn't have a specific starting point, what it does have is these—well, what I was referring to as "links." I mean, it's a "book" but in the virtual sense, there are "links." The bold-faced words that appear throughout the text, which are actually the titles of the entrees—so, while you're reading the text and you come across one of these bold-faced words, that's a word that has its own entree within *Arcanum*. So, although it needed to be A-to-Z, otherwise you'd be sitting there hunting through trying to figure out where the next section or reference would be.

But the purpose of it wasn't actually to be an "A-to-Z" reference. The purpose of it, was to have an integrated collection of related knowledge; that the facets could be cross-referenced easily.

A broad subject might bring up several dozen other elements that you might reference in order to have a better understanding of that subject or what the concept is. To do that—I mean, the book is already nearly one thousand pages long. And in doing that, I was able to eliminate one thousand pages because all of the information is interconnected; things don't need to be repeated in one section that have already been displayed in another. This has allowed me to present it as a complete master course in "magick" because of the way it is all-encompassing.

This doesn't mean it has every fact, figure, date and name that you could research or find in history or in some reference book somewhere; but it does provide all of the key material about where the concept of "magic"—as it's understood in contemporary "New Age" metaphysics—meets, for example, "magic" or other paradigms of "magic" or the "sciences" even, "Druidism," ancient Mesopotamia, even "systemology." I mean, really, it's kind of as they say: "The whole meal can be tasted within the first bit."

The purpose is not to be unnecessarily esoteric here—a person could definitely *flatten* and work out all the intricacies of using a "magical tradition" and still reach the higher points of actualization and realizations that we work with in Systemology.

However, without a "higher" level of understanding beyond just what is relayed verbatim at the core of magical materials and Druidry and so forth, the chances are that most practitioners and initiates actually aren't going to get to those realization points—and so most of them, they just kind of spend the rest of their time mulling about in those paradigms.

For some people, maybe that is the point that they've agreed to or decided to become fixed to for this lifetime. Maybe that's milestones ahead of where they've come from.

Now, a lot of the people we are finding that are dealing in Systemology and the high level work—these are people that, you know, metaphysically, esoterically, and it starts to get pretty fanciful for those that aren't ready to grasp or confront such levels of understanding or such concepts, but—these are people that have spent lifetimes in these pursuits; these are people who have literally been around the block many many times looking down these avenues and alleyways and traversing them back and forth and leaving breadcrumbs and beacons for themselves; and people that have even *been there present* when these traditions were alive and active—those that carry memory of different time periods, different cultures, different themes, or even put out or projected ahead of themselves that certain things would be left for them or beacons or what not... to recognize where they are on the *Pathway*...

I didn't create this Pathway...

I've recognized it; I've systematized it; I've... developed materials that I believe best represent what these degrees and levels and gradients are... But this is not my own creation. I'm simply systematizing it and bringing it into a communicable level of reality.

So, these are people now that have come to recognize different elements—whether it was from the "Necronomicon" or "Druidism" or "Magick" or "Occultism" and "Sorcery" and of course, our "Systemology" and they're like: "This is where I need to be" and this is where they are working at, and this is what's important. Because at a higher level, this *is*, of course, *what's important.*

Not everyone is going to be able to access it from this level—now, you got to wonder "why" sometimes, and that's one of the things that's uncovered later on. The individual that's strongly put off by owning a book with a pentagram on it, is obviously conditioned—or has reactive programming about that—since there's nothing inherently wrong with a piece of cardboard with some ink on it. Now, all of that other significance is given *by* Self. That is one of the key elements to a Master understanding of "magick" and mysticism and the mysteries, versus one that is just coming into it, getting Self-initiated or improperly trained, that fails to understand that Self *is* the one doing all this; Self is the *one* participating, creating the imagery, reacting to the imagery and then acting out in an objective universe.

This whole "energetic feedback relay system" of what we consider *Life* and the experience of the *Universe* and everything as our Reality—this is a participation point. And this participation point is generally referred to as "Will"— the "Will"—or else, the power of "Intention."

But specifically "Will"—and we see this word "Will" pop up quite frequently in the *old* esoteric texts; the one's that many people based these watered-down kind of traditions we see today being sold. But the oldest texts deal primarily with Will, and Will being the directive ability of Self to *create* energy and to *effect* the universe of space and time—and this is something that's lost in a lot of the more fluffy conventional "New Age" systems of "magick" and mysticism. This is something that we don't want our Seekers to succumb to.

There is a big draw now to the "magick" and the "mysteries" and the "fantasy" and what this could all mean—and even the "upper routes" to looking into ancient Europe and other traditions and cultures around the world, and Mesopotamia and our Systemology—there have always been the true Wizards and Mystics and individuals that represented these ideals.

However, what has been passed off in most cases today—particularly even in the underground, it's not just exclusive to the mainstream—is usually one more way of getting an individual sealed into one or another paradigm; one or another culture or pantheon of spirits or deities.

Seldom do we see a larger all-encompassing understanding come into it or a point where an individual is elevated up and beyond from those systems that they are working with. It becomes almost a matter of a "drug" on whether or not the individual is *using* the drug or the drug is *using* the individual.

There have always been possessors of hidden and occult knowledge. And there is also the organizations and materials and stuff that's available to you more readily that is really either fancy uses of psychology and basic principles of Hermetic or "New Thought" mixed with a lot of obscure symbolism and a lot of unnecessary trivial rigamarole that really does not contribute anything to developing someone further.

The real purpose of the magical tradition as studied with *The Great Magickal Arcanum* and *Sorcerer's Handbook* is to get an individual out of the patterned systems that they are used to.

So, they put on a new attire, a fanciful robe, they set up their own sacred space, they conduct themselves within this space, they give symbols and tools and iconic images certain meanings and significances which are then played with within this environment—and this is actually all very good "practice" for Self to begin to resume the power of Will and intention. All excellent... excellent ways of breaking away from old patterns and old reactivity and victimization and actually being at "cause" and at play in this universe.

The only danger is when this becomes the end-all be-all understanding for the individual.

And so once we can *flatten* this understanding of this concealed and secret knowledge—once we can open up the folds of these ancient mystery traditions—then we can lay it all out in the light and we can see it as it *is*. It no longer has any effect on us. It no longer has any control as "source" over us. We can see it for what it is. We can call it for what it *is*—create and destroy it as we need to, in regards to what we decide is effective for our own individual pathway and remove all that which does not survive the "acid-test" of effectiveness; that which liberates us to release and move on to higher levels of understanding.

: LECTURE 4—MASTERING MAGIC :
(September 21, 2020)

We have had at our disposal now an incredible wealth of Hermetic mysteries and philosophies to explore; many means of understanding the qualities of Cosmic Law. Finally, here with this last lecture of the day—I want to get into a higher understanding of what it means at a "Master" level to be dealing with the "Route of Magick and Mysticism."

We have to make certain we are not imposing any understanding that we have concerning this physical existence with that which is the All, or that which is Infinity; Any laws that may govern what we call the Alpha existence of a Spiritual Universe. Really, when you take the mystical work and the psychic phenomenon and magical rituals and other such efforts of practical metaphysics—they're really only effectively workable to the extent that we have certain agreements made concerning Cosmic Law and the Physical Universe.

Here is where, again, a Magician or a Master level practitioner must make certain that they understand that the power of what we consider "magic" *is* the power of "Will." Will put forth from Self. The I-AM. The directive force in the Physical Universe concerning our reality; concerning what you are experiencing. Because your point of view may be fixed here at this moment to a physical incarnation or occupying a space within this room, yet the real essence and Spirit and the Being of I-AM or Self occupies this "higher" reality.

This cannot be dismissed no matter what level or grade we are working at. Otherwise we might fall prey to the trappings of those individual grades which somehow put an emphasis on the knowledge or the accumulation of the facts that will make a specific paradigm function and work. Whatever semantics being used is acceptable.

Now, we chose the word "ZU" to represent the Life, the Lifeforce, the Spirit and the Self, based on a very very ancient form of semantics, because it was the oldest written semantics that we have to work with; the oldest languages of written records. Otherwise, we have thousands of years afterward of various interpretations of that knowledge under various guises and paradigms—all of which are explorable; all of which we can simply *flatten* the mystery of by exploring properly at the grade of "magick and mysticism," therefore basically eliminating the sense of mystery, the "unknown" factor—that there is anything hiding under these rocks, or that to basically eliminate what I have found to be the case of many that dwell far too long on the lunar level.

It's a gamblers fallacy—that just *one more* pull of that level is going to produce the result. And this is... again, a trapping of the grade. And so what we are dealing with—we are dealing with real Gate Walking in the Master Course and the grades that we're presenting; the real piercing of the veils. This is not the kind of stuff you just read about in planetary grimoires, or conducting ceremonies every full moon or what not—these are all elements and tools that can be used to reach higher levels of realization, but one of the issues that we find is, again, this "gambler's fallacy" of one more "grimoire"; one more "magick notebook"; just one more "spell" that can be uncovered—you know, it's... they're still looking for an "effect."

They're looking to be the effect and not cause an effect. And this is the main trapping of magick and mysticism. You don't see this as much in Druidism as we move into the other half of the grade, because there the Self is being put in connection with the environment more directly—in Nature,

And Nature as we know, it seems to be there almost as a permanency. We're not the ones... It's there when we arrive on the planet and it's there when we go, type thing. And so we're starting to move Self into an environment and look at the environment.

The danger there being, of course, that unless we conduct, you know, the right words under the right type of species of tree and so on, that we can't access some mystery and so forth... We see these trappings really all along the way—anything that moves the emphasis away, of course, from what we've referred to as "Self-Honesty" and being in a point of Self-Awareness that is not restricted to one or another ideal or paradigm or restriction.

Those parameters... now you can freely decide to do whatever you choose to do; but how can it be a "free decision" while those parameters are still in place. There's things you can freely decide *not* to do, but the reactivity concerning what *is* actually *within* the parameters is what's going to define that. As I say: the upper most limit of what we are doing with the Master Course is really making a more able and creative individual.

And of course, as I say: that's limited to the extent of one's imagination: one's ability to imagine or call to mind—which of course means to "summon" up a mental image and actually be able to confront it and be okay with it; there's a lot of things that people are conditioned or have conditioned themselves to not want to look at.

With magick and mysticism that's one of the first aspects of the *lunar veil*—is to suddenly be able to have a much more wider encompassing view; regardless of how that's being processed or what semantics are being used to represent it. Now, we're mostly concerned with pretty much the highest level we can reach in using these fundamentals, but sometimes that is too steep of a gradient to throw at an individual; to throw them, for example, the *Systemology Handbook* or

Tablets of Destiny, if they don't already have any foundation on which to place that information, that understanding. It kind of comes out of the blue then, all of a sudden, and it doesn't seem very real, and so it doesn't seem very accessible and they're less likely to reach for it and what it represents and to actually effectively employ it.

When we represent the grades, for example, Grade-I with "Magick and Mysticism" we are not really enforcing that all Mardukite Zuists, for example, or all Systemologists, or everyone that comes through the Mardukite Academy, be required to study and practice "Magick and Mysticism" as relayed in Route-I (Route-A). Now, if you are looking for a "Master" level understanding; if you want to be "certified" as an "instructor"; you want to be a "Master Mardukite" in terms of the significance of what it represents as a finite fixed point that we've established for what realizations and ability and knowledge and so forth are accessible within these three Grades, well, then yeah, we want you to have a full working understanding of "magical" and "occult" semantics as they've applied for the last 2500 years, because they crop up here and there. And also to eliminate the "mystery."

When we start talking about the more—the less—ritualistic occult and rigid practices from the older, like Grade-II Mesopotamian tradition, we still see correspondences and we see many procedures, but a much more fluid relationship with the universe and the cosmos. And a person should be able to differentiate between the "holy magics" as they were relayed, or the "religious magics," or the practices and purposes as they are relayed in "Mardukite Zuism" if they are going to use that as a quasi-religious expression in modern times—in comparison to how these facets have been explored, practiced and laid down in the past; because that is the working understanding we had until this point.

Up until Systemology about a year ago, we've really only had the old works to draw from—and that's a little bit more of a shared reality than when we get to Grade-III where we are dealing with our new semantics and we are dealing with our more wide encompassing universal applications of vocabulary that encompasses not only Grade-III Systemology, but applies to all of the foundational levels beneath it that have led to that understanding.

Now, it would be, of course, my hope that an individual would just fall into Zuism or Systemology, for example, and the practices and processing and basically reach farther and farther up the *Pathway*. There's no reason a person *has* to be brought back to Grade-I in order to work forward. However, as I say: this being a reconstruction of the "Ancient Mystery School" that we are operating as the Mardukite Academy, this is an all-encompassing knowledge. And if we want a full comprehension of where things were, how things can be, where things are going, this is what we provide to the extent that an individual is willing to reach for it; that's all we can ever provide.

The enforcement and indoctrination of instruction really, you know, here in the Mardukite Master Course that might be applicable to instructors and Masters because we want to make sure we are all on the same page here when we are delivering this information in the name of the this movement all around the world. That there is a concise systematized structure that we are all following and that an individual that has gone through the "Magick School" at some lodge of the Mardukite Academy in Canada or France or Australia, that it's going to be comparably the same to what would be delivered, for example, here at our main offices, or to the extent that an individual is going to understand it working through the materials and listening to these original course recordings of the Master Course as *I* deliver it, which of course, is a little bit different.

I'm gearing these (lectures) toward a Master level understanding for those that have worked through the materials or are going to be actively working through the material while listening to these (lectures) in lieu of the fact that I can actually deliver the course more widely this way from the source and individuals can either pick it up on their own to study it at their own leisure at home or as part of one of the Academy lodges or schools or Zuist churches of the Mardukite Tradition that we plan to establish.

This is actually a milestone achievement for us—with these Master Editions—because we have not been able to reach this level of duplication before; and also the wider reach of our materials. Most of our materials were originally underground (publications). So, really what we want to do is bring people to a high level understanding, a workable understanding, of the various degrees and levels and how they work together, and how things came to be what they are.

There are many other methods that can be used in addition to this; if an individual instructor wishes to employ their "processing"—if they are a *Pilot*—or those that wish to demonstrate the procedures of "processing" at least to the extent that they are relayed in Grade-III... we're not mixing "Piloting Procedure" or any of the higher "Metahuman Systemology" into the "Master Course." As I say: we've finally been able to reach a pinnacle point where we could draw the line of Grade-III and finally reach the goals that we had set out to achieve for that.

Now, there's a lot of "processing"—particularly the "objective processing"—which involves using Systemology and the relationship with the external world, that really kind of goes hand in hand with older "ritual" techniques. Just as I didn't create the *Pathway* and the actual knowledge itself—I collected and systematized it. And once I reach the extent of the paradigms in the past; reach the extent that—here is what the "Druid" systematization is, here is "Mesopotamia," here is what the "Western Magical Tradition" and so forth—it really was about: what does this all add up to and what does this all mean, and what is the actual points that these are all trying to reach at an almost universalist level?

We are not taking the approach, as some have in the past, that well, "they are all correct." Or—"well, they all have elements of being correct...meanwhile, we'll just accept them all as they are" and so on and so forth. That's all fine and good if you want to interact with people on the street and not have to engage in some kind of conflict or something of that nature because of reactivity or emotional ties, but that really doesn't have much to do with what the actual Truth of how things are—which, it cannot be restricted to one set of semantics or another.

So at the very least, the material within these grades—the "Route of Magick and Mysticism," the "Route of Druidism" and "Mesopotamia"—they suggest very specific models and "kabbalahs" and systematized pathways that really do form a structure that we haven't completely departed from as we move up into Grade-III Systemology and, well, beyond.

The models and scales, the ZU-line, the charts—everything we've done in our higher level work, including Grade-III, is really built upon that basis, that foundation. That's why we express it the way we do. And it's not necessarily "necessary" of course, as a prerequisite to understanding our Systemology because, the Systemology that we've developed encompasses the rest of it in a very simplistic, straightforward and direct manner.

However it doesn't deal with the older semantics; doesn't deal with the older cultural ideals and mythologies to a great extent. There *are* ancient "kabbalahs" and forms of systematizing "World Trees" and the "Universes" and ways to relay the relationship that Self has, depending on its point of view or its reference as Self, with all of these existences.

Now, unfortunately, we haven't found that they are all necessarily workably effective in getting the individual to higher points of realization; higher Self-Actualization; actually accessing these higher veils towards what we are considering "Ascension" because that's an accepted term of it, but it's not so much of... we *are* these spiritual beings that operate far and beyond *this* physical, and what we consider "Beta" existence. We *are* these "Alpha" beings. And it is only a matter of considerations and many lifetimes of restrictions, the solidity of belief and fixed realities, that's brought us to these lower points by accumulating more and more of these false barriers; more and more of these false images we carry around; more and more stores of emotional ties and energies that have kept us from achieving the freedom that is accessible as the Human Spirit.

Those higher vistas we are now considering, for example, "Wizard" level—or "metahuman"—and "Actualized Technician." These are terms now being thrown around in the Systemology Society that pertain to Grade-IV and above. Now, the whole point of this is not some raceway; the point of this is not "oh, well, first you go through Grade-I, and then we give you this little piece of paper, and you go through Grade-II, and the whole point of that is to go to Grade-III." That's not what we are trying to do; we are not trying to repeat the false intention and emphasis of former educational systems—that's not our purpose here.

The grading was simply a way of actually plotting knowledge and what was actual *with* that knowledge, and real, as potential realizations, at each step of the way. And what is most accessible and what is within reach. It's a lot easier to work this stuff on a gradient scale. So, the point is not, again, to enforce that we push every single grade. But these classes of instruction do exist here for a reason.

Really to get the most, for example, from the "Route of Druidism," then the "Route of Magick and Mysticism" is of extraordinary benefit. And then of course, to understand, to put, Grade-II into a perspective that Western Civilization can be understand, the "Route of Druidry" that we use sometimes as a "bridge" specifically, deals, pertains, exclusively with the concept that: here's Druidry; here's Druidry as we understand it, and then when we look back into the origins of Druidry, we find ourselves in Mesopotamia. It is very helpful, especially given that, for example, a lot of the material in *Merlyn's Complete Book of Druidism: A Master Course in Druidry for Modern Druids—Elvenomicon* and *Draconomicon*—that material was originally used when we founded the "Mardukites" and what is now considered the basis for Grade-II material.

Now, there were many people that came into our fray that their first point of contact and entry-point was the "Necronomicon" or was the "Anunnaki" or "Mesopotamia" and then after working through that, they went back and they went: "oh, well, this is all very good material and I like this presentation"—they go back and they look at the Druid material and they start to work their way back through the grades down to establish that foundation simply for a greater sense of certainty and again to eliminate the "mystery"—this walking perpetually of "why," "why," "why"—and, you know "chicken before the egg"; and work out enough of this to be certain that there is enough foundation to simply move forward.

This does not mean we are rushing people through the grades to move forward; this means that there *is* all of the certainty and foundation and everything quite accessible as an Ancient Mystery Tradition, to bring someone up through these grades and have them accessing more and more within their reach by standing on ledges of true Knowingness and not just accepting things on faith.

There's really very little here—as we work through, if you have the proper understanding of what's taking place, even with all the fanciful presentations of "magick" and mysticism and what have you—that requires a lot of "faith." What it really requires is "understanding."

We're not too concerned with just taking beliefs on faith, because that's a solidity of somebody else's reality.

What is most important is what is within the grasp of an individual to actually experience for themselves. And to understand what is happening; what is at "cause"; what "effects" are taking place; how these relationships are being communicated—and then, if they want to put a lot of colorful semantics and vocabulary onto the type of energetic exchanges taking place, or the classification of certain attributes, that's all fine and good. What we don't want to do is restrict our understanding to *only* these systematic patterns of "magickal correspondences" and so forth—spirit sigils and planetary alignments; all of it is only useful and workable to, as a successful path, to the extent that it's carrying somebody forward.

Let us not rush Seekers through the grades, but one should expect—I've synthesized quite a bit of material here over the course of twenty-five years. Now, it is now accelerating, because that's how it seems to work: as more of this has come together, more of it *has* come together, and continues to come together—and we've been able to reach much farther now than ever before, ever even conceived of when standing at these lower ledges of realty, which seemed like incredible vistas and monumental turning points as they rightfully were. But in this instance, we're simply classifying each of those as a "grade" and not treating it as anything other than what that is.

And they are incredible "vistas" and "monuments" of human understanding and collected wisdom and information that can propel us forward. But much as we don't want meandering and wandering too long at lunar levels, we've also discovered the hidden—what's behind the screens of for example, Mardukite Zuism and the ancient Babylonian and Mesopotamian tradition and the Anunnaki traditions and the Arcane Tablets, what they lead to; and that ultimately led us to Systemology.

And so really, one of the benefits in studying and exploring the full extent of the Mardukite Master Course is the ability to relay and understand all of these levels as it goes along; to understand the relationship, for example, that the "Druid's Cabala" or the "Ladder of Lights"—the Babylonian "StarGates"—the background of the "Semitic Kabbalah" or any of these paradigms; the "Chakras," various interpretations of "Selfs" or "Bodies" that have been compounded or overlapped; how all of the ways these mystical expressions have been relayed in the past, can be synthesized, refined, better understood, better applied today in our Systemology. But once after looking at them for what they were and what they are; not just solely going into Systemology and saying: "well, we have this 'ZU-line' and this 'standard model' and it all seems to work fine within this..."

No, let's actually look at the things that led up to this point and that even myself, you know, I can't take full credit for creating the "Standard Model" and the "Zu-line" and the "Scales" that Systemology is now very much accelerating its success on, because these are all very very *old*, very commonly dispersed throughout the esoteric underground and "New Age" traditions and so forth—But!—without getting beyond the semantics or gaining a wider view or unifying understanding, which is definitely accessible even within Grade-I material.

These individuals had a tendency to just simply cling on to these individual paradigms and what their symbolism and significances had been ascribed, without seeing anything further and any further applications. And this would be all fine and good, had any of the former traditions that we have based our Systemology—had any of them actually reached definitively and with good ability to duplicate between apprenticeships spanning thousands of years, the type of goals that we wanted to reach with what we define as the Master Course or the Master Grades.

We would have simply compounded upon those to their "nth" degree. Since we were not able to do that, it required developing a new "NexGen" or "futurist" understanding, which we can represent for those that need to have some sense of systematized symbolism and structure in terms of a mythology and some kind of grasp with the ancient history that we *can* observe, as Mardukite Zuism and the ancient Mesopotamian traditions, but going much farther to establish a new Systemology; a new higher understanding of all that has come before and all that could still be within Mardukite Systemology.

[*I want to thank you now for being here today, and I we'll have you back tomorrow with a new set of lectures.*]

: LECTURE 5—THE MAGIC SCHOOL :
(September 22, 2020)

Alright, I want to welcome you all back this morning—this is September the 22nd we have here; and on the itinerary, it shows I got ya for five hours, which will allow four hours of lecture plus breaks. And... according to our schedule, we are to talk about Grade-I "Magic Schools," which is always something of significant interest. It's... you know, we covered a little bit about entering people onto the levels and the gradients and the entry-points yesterday—in yesterday's lectures.

So today we are talking about "Magic Schools"—*your* "Magic School" representing the Mardukite Master Course, the Mardukite Academy, any of your local lodges or chapters, courses that might be offered through a chapter or a Church of (Mardukite) Zuism. So... let's really just get right into this.

Magic Schools: we've got really, you know... magic has been separated into a lot of factions and divisions these days. We've kind of divided—in Grade-I, you see we have "Cycle-A" and "Cycle-D" and "Route-A" and "Route-D" in terms of the literature and the training and general magic of the *Arcanum* material, and then of course an emphasis on European magic in the form of Druidism...and its ties into the former Mesopotamian tradition.

So what that gives you—you have a lot of various magicians, sorcerers, we've got witchcraft, we've got Druidry, shamanism would fall within that parameter of Grade-I... all these various titles and so forth. Technically—when we released *Arcanum*, we wanted to make sure that things were cohesive for its release in terms of publishing and the way books are set up and titled and so forth, so we called it a *Master Course in Magick for Modern Wizards.* As you know, here in the Academy and in Systemology, we treat the "Wizard" levels as Grade-IV and above as "Wizard Grades." Below: we're dealing with "Master Grades."

To be a "Master Magician" then, would be probably more accurate—and we, we're not really concerned with gender titles in this, you know: "druid" or "druidess"; a "witch" or "warlock"... that's all stuff that kinda gets *flattened* out in Grade-I as a Seeker explores all the various parameters and divisions of what constitutes as "magick"—what constitutes as "magick" using the semantics of, perhaps, the "Druidic" or perhaps an "Earth-oriented" tradition or "Wicca" versus "High Magic," "ceremonial magic," works of the "Golden Dawn," and Israel Regardie, Aleister Crowley and so forth.

There's really only *one* magic. And the fundamental of magic, if we want to break it down, is "energy" right? I mean, that's what we are dealing with at every point, and the interesting thing is that as we move farther and farther along this course, up the Grades, you're dealing mainly still with just *energy.* But its—how is it being understood; how is it being treated; these things change as we are moving up the grades, until we are really just dealing with energies as they are found in their blatant raw flow and cycles and generations and all of that at the Alpha levels—the Alpha Spirit generating energies, generating viewpoints, generating mental imagery.

Nothing really changes except our refinement and our understanding of the practice and our involvement and participation in this as we move up the grades. So, even if you are working with, you know—for over two decades now—if you've been working with the *Sorcerer's Handbook*, I've started each edition the same way: the "Core of Magic" opens with the section on energy and the blanket statement that "it exists in all things; it's the driving force behind all magic." So there it is.

You're dealing with *energy*. Everything else is secondary to that. In "magick" we tend to deal a lot with symbols; and we deal a lot with representations. In "sympathetic magic"—the concept of "sympathetic magic" which is almost as old as, more of an anthropological scientific term—but in that, we use representations of something as they are connected to something else. So, for example, you have a piece of "hair" from somebody, so that has their—well, we know now that hair actually has genetic material.

When we consider—when we look back at—these old grimoires, and they say "oh, collect pieces of hair, fingernails..." certain things like that, articles of clothing that may contain sweat; an individual's blood... we look at that *now* and we see that maybe that's not so ridiculous, because there *is* definitely an energetic connection, if we were to give it the significance of one, between having those types of articles and then, of course, the ways in which those are used or implemented: the belief that by having those types of articles, there is a certain power, or a certain connection that may be demonstrated.

Therefore, an energetic flow can be connected—a communication of energies can be connected—presumably across distances. Because presumably the way we see space and time in this universe, we are of course, dealing with only agreements concerning material physical universe as they're affected here. And that's one of the things you need to understand with magic, because "magick" is most often a concern of affecting as things are in the physical universe. So you are dealing with a collision of two universes there.

You're dealing with universe of the magician and you're dealing with the physical universe, the agreed upon universe in which they've chosen to inhabit—or been enforced or enslaved or however we want to look at this later on in the gradients—to inhabit the point of view *of* a physical body, a genetic vehicle, an incarnation within the physical universe.

Whether they be "magicians" or ... That's all about the Will and knowledge and aptitude of the Self—the Seeker—has nothing to do with the physical body. The physical body is simply the means in which we are using to communicate in a physical universe as agreed upon with other physical bodies are used as point of views for other identities.

It doesn't mean we are actually entrapped into this universe; only our point of view and our considerations during the degradation of lifetimes and beliefs and all of the conditioning—implants and imprinting—that's taken place. We've come now down to this lower level of understanding, and this lower level of being and this lower level of confining our point of view down here in order to interact and communicate with this existence that's taking place.

So, we must always keep these elements in mind if we are going to have this higher "Master" understanding of Grade-I work; otherwise we would still just treat Grade-I work as the end-all be-all and it's all "magic schools" and nothing can be beyond that and nothing came before and nothing could be understood from cuneiform tablets and there is nothing new we can take this to in the future and we would basically just have a persistent piece of knowledge that would actually probably degrade, since it's not bringing us any farther, what would tend to happen is *that* knowledge, as we continue to chart across time, would continue to degrade and what we would be left with is lower and lower points of consideration. Which is what we see.

This is what we see the direction happening when those individuals are not moving up and out into higher plateaus of Awareness; a higher point of Actualized Awareness, ledges of knowing and what we demonstrate as the grades go forward. So, as a Master, yes, we're going to still be offering "Magic Schools" because, just as you or I or another individual might have best been introduced or use this as an entry-point to get out of the Earth Gate and to begin to consider more possibilities and potential for Self—we're not going to exclude this.

However, we've done so much more research, discovery, experimentation, the development of Systemology and its processing methods and so forth, that we need to not forget that we are still coming from a higher perspective in looking at this now.

So long as we aren't overwhelming Seekers at an educational level, but basically when it comes to the Mardukite Master Course as *I* deliver it to you, and any of these grades as they're divided or brought to curriculum based courses at your lodges or personal apprenticeships—everything within the course, Grade-I through (*three*) is pretty much fair game here as an understanding and to be pulled from, so long as we don't start going into Systemology Piloting or Piloted Processing.

Everything up until that point, which includes material from *Tablets of Destiny* and *Crystal Clear*—all of these points of understanding, this is expected for a Master to understand so that in relaying the "Core of Magick" here or the "Witchcraft Traditions" or any of these lower steps that people that need to receive this knowledge, understand it, get it *flattened*, not be reactive to it, not have it trip them up or be stuck in it in any way, and to be able to moved passed those paradigms into higher points of understanding.

It's also necessary for the Pilot to fully understand both the viewpoint *of* the Seeker that's at that level of understanding, but also not lost their place and their point on the *Pathway* in staying involved with these subjects. Because that's something we've noticed—that a lot of Systemologists actually, as the routes have gone on, have done. Which is fine as a personal path; you've been through it, you want to shed it and move up—keep working on personal development—that's encouraged, that's what this is all about.

Now, of course, with the Mardukite Academy, with the Founding Church of Mardukite Zuism, with our Society of Systemology, we're concerned also the delivery of this information to a point beyond just myself. You know—beyond just myself as a Founder or Originator or Author or... sitting up in some Ivory Tower somewhere just speaking to you guys or a handful of individuals online and so on, because the materials themselves have a far reach now. We have large global distribution with our printed material than ever before.

The higher level understanding should follow with that—and the personal instruction, the relay of information and much more candid fluid higher points of understanding, such as the Mardukite Master Course which can't really be duplicated in the printed word. We can later go back and release these as transcripts, but it's not the same as hearing it, being able to register it, looking at the books first and then getting someone or like myself or one of our other instructors to give overviews of various things, or answers questions—which I do encourage during this course period.

[If you could write down, those of you that are present here, because we are recording these (lectures)—if you could write down the questions about the materials at each grade as we are working through it, and then in next lectures, I can kind of relay that out to everybody. Because I think a "Q-and-A" here with the microphone would be really hard to pick up. So... If we could do it that way.]

Now, so the "Core of Magick"—we deal with energy... it's first and foremost in the *Sorcerer's Handbook*, and honestly all through the grades, that's what we are dealing with is "energy." We're never really departing from that. And more importantly we are trying to get the Seeker to basically *break* more and more of their agreements of reality concerning the physical universe and those being the *only* considerations for how things can be.

This is only one universe. And we know that we are occupying it as a point of view from a higher point of Awareness somewhere else. We know that; we've been able to establish that in even traditional "magic" although the semantics get gray. We've been able to find it on the most ancient cuneiform tablets, but it's probably best presented in our newer version of NexGen and Mardukite "Systemology."

I mean almost a year ago, when I presented the "Power of Zu" lectures, which are in the "Instructor's Manual" of the "Master Course" (Instructor's Edition)—the same principle was being applied. We were trying to understand a way of unifying our presentation of this, because what we are now calling "Zu"—and of course "Zuism" being named for that—that is just one semantic for that, but it was a good one and it was an old one.

What it represented was a way of very simply defining this spiritual energy continuum and Lifeforce that extends from Self; that Self projects out from its remote Alpha-Spirit point, in which to engage and reach and develop and manifest and apply energies and efforts to existence—to what we know as Reality.

And so "Zu" is a—it's what in former Systemology presentations nearly a decade ago, we were calling it a "monistic continuum." And the concept of a "monistic continuum" is that you have a singular "force" which simply has varying degrees of manifestation and expression based on the interactions at those various degrees. So, it's not that the energy itself is changing—the Zu energy, the Identity of Self, Actualized Awareness being sent out to have an experience, to project, to receive, to accept and reject, to reach and withdraw—this is all coming from virtually a static point.

Then you see this expression of Self or Spirit—or however you want to call it—you see this condensing and changing as it extends itself towards the, well, physical point of view, in our case. Since we are still kind of occupying these physical bodies as a point of view; a point of view only. Because we know better than to say that we are these bodies.

So, what are we dealing with? We're dealing with an "Alpha Spirit" and then we have what it directs in a spiritual domain or a spiritual dimension or a spiritual universe—okay —as its own prime thought, its own directive thought in a completely raw and spiritually energetic form; which is then expressed downward as "Will"—the "Willpower."

Willpower is what engages the "Mind-System" as being a directive causative point of view and source, okay? So, now we have "Willpower" and the "Mind-System." The "Mind-System" is not only attached to—not only what you carry with you between lives, but also the systems of how you've operated this particular one. So, we consider the "Mind-System" now, part of the "Beta Universe," which is the "Physical Universe."

The Mind-System may not be as solid as the solidification and concentration of energy particles as, for example, this table—but, we are dealing with a "Beta Existence" at that juncture. The Mind is mainly there to determine or gauge or evaluate the amount of effort that is needed and how it is to be applied to get or result in the right effect at the physical universe level; because that's what we're here changing— particularly at the "magick" level.

I mean, although people speak of "Ascension"—we talk of "holy magic" and "high magick"—at the magical level, we're still pretty much concerned with the material universe. And for some, that's a good step—that's a big gradient to just get up to at a point of Cause in the physical universe, because obviously this is a game-field that we are very much working with.

Now, when it comes to the classification of energy, this is where things start to get murky—and this is where the "Master" and "instructors" really come in handy in keeping a Seeker on track, unified understanding of energies. Because in one place, they're going to be reading a lot or learning a lot about "light," "rays of light," the "lights"—whether it's an astral light, spiritual light, Divine light... "Light." It comes up a lot.

Any type of energy—anywhere where subtle energies or universal energies, cosmic ener... anytime the term "energy" is even blatantly used—they're... when you deal with certain forms of "Ascension" they talk a lot about the "God Mind," "Divine Sparks," "God-Force"—things of that nature.

Each language, depending on whether you're dealing the Semitic Kabbalah, you're dealing with Babylon, the Druids... each language classifies its own observance of this same type of energy in its own way, and there are some that have still not come to the unified understanding that this is—we are speaking of the same spiritual energy or the same vital energies regardless of paradigm. And this is really really important.

If you keep Grade-I fragmented—see, the purpose of Grade-I isn't necessarily to show in *Arcanum* how widely dispersed we can make all of this knowledge and keep it dispersed. The purpose of it was unification, pure and foremost. The concepts of "magick"—the ones that work—you know, the nitty gritty of "magick" that is actually effective and workable and actually serves a function—continues to serve a function—as you move up the grades, it isn't just something that: "well, that was useful at one point, but it's no longer..."

The true heart of it all is really very simple—and is really what we're trying to break down here as a Master Course or in analyzing Grade-I, now from a systemological level... blatantly. I mean we've talked of magic systems before. We've talked of taking systematic approaches. But, now the completion of Grade-III and the Master Course—there's no excuses. There is just no excuses for lower levels of understanding to be held onto in that respect. [*laughs*]

That's one of the things we're going to be confronting here and one of the things you've already dealt with in overcoming certain mental barriers and programming barriers and so forth, is again, breaking those agreements with the physical universe, the material universe, the programming of it, the understanding of it that has been conditioned from the physical sciences... Because don't forget we're going into two directions here.

We're going into the direction of where we are moving into a "more than human," "metahuman," "Alpha spiritual" point of development in our Systemology and our Zuism. And that is in complete conflict with the solidity and concrete nature of material sciences, which are anything *but* imaginative. Although they may have started on some very curious and philosophical premises, they became way more narrowed down and condensed as time went on.

Like painting a canvas: you're working with the canvas; and at first, there really... it's just a free form. Anything goes. You start to create a little bit of a form; you start to shape things in a certain way—decide that you're going to pinpoint: "well, now this is going to be the basic form of a tree, and maybe we'll put a building over there." Now, you may not have solidified this form entirely yet, but you have begun to place parameters on what something is going to be. The potential of that once infinite Beingness—and now we are going to create some kind of form.

And that is what we see handled more and more when a practitioner is operating with magic. What are they operating with? We've talked briefly so far about energy, but what else are they operating with? What's the other aspect of the Mi... Mental image pictures. Imagery. Imagination. The visualization. That's it!

You've got visualization, you've got energy, you've got the Awareness of the individual connecting the two... that's it! I mean, that's "magic" in a nutshell.

Now, I just as easily say, "that's it" and we'll all go home. But obviously, even that basic understanding is not very unique or original—we've had these kind of premises and axioms set before us in the past. But what we're trying to do is work our way up a pattern of workability, effectiveness—something that's practical. And for those that the gradient scale of just "creating prime thought" or "Alpha Thought" or "postulating" or simply willing into being that things are a certain way, you're feeling a certain way—suddenly, you're going to decide "I'm going to be a different way" or your interacting with something and suddenly you're reacting and you're feeling all this programming triggering up inside you and so on... and you say, you know, "I see that, and I'm going to not succumb to that. I'm not going to be the effect of some program or some conditioned set of patterned behaviors or thought trails that has dictated that, while the next time this happens this is my associated knowledge with that and I know what that is..." and so on.

Because that... that's basically what we are doing at the material level—the physical universe level, is we've basically come up with the lowest level or the lowest common denominator of beliefs and agreements to create a solid existence of—beta-existence—to share communications in. And this is the lowest common denominator. And this has not been the lowest common denominator always, you see?

There is a downward kind of trail—or slide—that seems to take place as societies and existences, each lifetime, the cultures, the way in which the universe is treated as *real*. And it's becoming more and more and more solid. And that's only a result of the Awareness and attention and persistence that is placed upon it, because we can't really even be certain that—even at the physical science levels—of cosmology and astronomy and so forth, that we actually understand the backbone behind this universe from a physical science level.

We have a better chance of that by moving our Awareness

points *outside* of this universe, than we do in using any of these instruments and the type of calculations and observations that are fixed and confined to specific scientific parameters to understand. We don't know that this universe was even *created* in a physical sense or actually being *Willed*... Willed into being and kept in persistence by *our* participation; by *our* ability to interact with it and direct forces within it from this perspective.

You're directing your Awareness into this body; and from that you are looking outward and interacting with energies and you have been conditioned from birth about forms, about shapes, about colors, about the significances, distance, time... And to say that these things are an "illusion" now—which is a slippery slope, I must say. There are a lot of magical paths that will do that... and *that* removes full responsibility, full ability to command or control, and full ability to know or do, within those domains; and you then become the effect of.

So, that's something to keep in mind—which is why I express this lecture and we're approaching "Magic School" in this kind of "high refined" systemological and intellectual way. Because you have to keep this other element in mind too: that these systems are also spiritual traps.

That these levels and these gradients were each meant to confine a certain understanding and as we move farther back, we see a wider understanding and wider understanding. And as we look from the most current "magical applications" and grimoires of the last few hundred years and traditions—we've become more refined and systematic with it, more rigid in terms of "magical correspondences," the associations and so forth.

And that's the type of stuff that we uncover in Grade-I, because we need to *flatten* those. We need to *flatten* the understanding that things have de-evolved to this point.

When we look previous to that—what they were actually based on—for example, in Mesopotamia and what we uncover in Grade-II, we don't find as much rigidity; we don't find as much... very specific points that have to be met in terms of ability. And there we see more "Divine" practice; we see "prayer"; we see a "communication" still taking place between something that is "outside" this environment, which may have been represented at some point by physical deities, which may have later been represented at some point by more human priests and priestesses and then de-evolved into our systems of government and so on.

But in the beginning, it wasn't—it was not nearly as refined and as rigid and structured. Although there was definitely a systematization at play, but the considerations for that systematization were not nearly as fixed to the symbolism, which is about all they were able to hold onto once considerations dropped down another level thereafter. As we enter the period—the more classical periods—the Grecco-Roman, even the more, the Neo-Babylonian period of Nebuchadnezzar and the rise of the Jewish traditions and the Kabbalah and the development of ceremonial magic as it ended up entering into the Medieval periods later—we see way more calculations, refinements, structures, rules, correspondences and all of which, if they aren't met, lead to invalidating that the individual has the ability to create change in accordance with Will for this physical existence.

And at the end of the day, we know that that really is all that magick is. And we can basically work from these fundamentals: that energy is everything; magic is basically the understanding and use of energy; control and command of it. Mastering magic has to do with breaking agreements with the material universe, the physical "Beta" universe as it stands, as it has been agreed to as a commonality. Then also being able to apply Will; apply energy to direct the changes that are desired in this existence.

And if you can do all that, you have "magick."

: LECTURE 6—FUNDAMENTALS OF MAGIC :
(September 22, 2020)

So now we say—basically—"magic is creating change in accordance with Will," right? That's what... when we boil it down: creating change with an understanding of energies in a way that conventional science, perhaps, has not fully understood. It's funny because this is really the basic definition that was being carried through the 20th century.

We quote Aleister Crowley the most (in the New Age) but we're pretty sure he dug it up either from Eliphas Levi or something from the Golden Dawn...or, you know, Levi probably got it from reading Francis Barrett's the *Magus*, which of course is a plagiarization of Agrippa's *Three Books of Occult Philosophy*...and so on.

Tracking down the origins of "magic"—I mean we can talk about the "History of Magic" later because I'm sure that's something of interest. But, we're talking about really a breakdown understanding of what's effective in "magick." A lot of this stuff has passed hands for quite some time; individuals to individuals—and it's hard to even say what we can credit for what.

We know that Crowley was already, you know, a quite established magician—but his involvement with the Golden Dawn and then the later, basically, plagiarized Golden Dawn tradition in the formation of his own versions of that and presenting it as, you know, in his flavor...

It becomes difficult to track down some of the most critical operations as they emerged in the 20th century; things that we now take for granted; operations that are collected in the *Sorcerer's Handbook* even, and of course, *Arcanum*.

What we do want to make sure is—that the Seeker has at least an understanding of energy. We don't really want to overwhelm our "Magic Schools" with Grade-III understandings and teachings and what not, because obviously this is practiced on a gradient scale. But we do want to make sure there is a universalist understanding of energy free of any particular semantics or traditions or the way in which a "Thelemite"—which is actually named for the word "Will" and traditionally is a name of a practitioner or follower of Aleister Crowley's work—that they might use semantics different, or operations different, from, for example, what Aurum Solis and the magical philosophies of that tradition or Theosophy or any of them.

Each have presented their own traditions in which each have their own flavors. The Rosicrucians being another one, very closely tied to both Freemasonry in some respects, and also the Golden Dawn and so on, and also Theosophy and so on. All of which share a unique trail, however they got their particular flavor of material, whatever culture or cultural pantheon of deities or mythology they have decided to emphasize.

Previous to the Mardukite movement, most of these traditions emphasized Egypt. Now, you do see a Grecco-Roman basic pagan mythology and basically a revival of any and all cultures appear in modern neopaganism, modern Wiccan traditions—and even then, you see a lot of differences between Wiccan or neopagan traditions mainly due to the culture that they may observe or the particular practice in which they decided to receive their information.

For example, in Wicca, we have Alexandrian Wicca; we have Gardnerian Wicca. Hardly either one is practiced verbatim anymore in today's society. They've all become either ingrained into or a part of someone else's tradition. One emphasized the more traditional folk witchcraft tradition; the other brought it more elements of ceremonial magic, such as you find with the grimoires of the *Key of Solomon* and so forth.

So, we have multiple approaches—even within Grade-I, which is why *all* of that is considered Grade-I. It doesn't matter whether we are dealing with traditional witchcraft, conventional Wicca, Druidism, creative visualization, candle meditations, operations of the Golden Dawn and ceremonial magic, enochian magic—anywhere where a ritual circle is drawn, cast, with very specific parameters and usually by either a solitary practitioner or a "coven" or "grove" or "circle" or group that is operating toward similar goals, and which is all initiated into its own unique little niche—to be on the same page.

So these are all applications of the magical tradition as you would find it in any of the literature; specifically in ours, the Grade-I materials—the *Sorcerer's Handbook* and *Arcanum*, which are now combined in the new *Arcanum*. The *Sorcerer's Handbook* is still available as a stand-alone handbook; but it was appropriate for our Master Course—Grade-I Route-A—for this new edition of *The Great Magickal Arcanum: A Master Course in Magick for Modern Wizards.* We now include the full text of the *Sorcerer's Handbook* as an "Introduction" to that to give some structure, which can then be expanded upon throughout the later course text of *Arcanum.*

Basically find—when you're delivering magic in your schools or your apprentice—find the niche that appeals to them most. It's very possible that those are a beacon or a symbol or something that was directed ahead of them as a way of being "clued-in" to the *Pathway*, and getting involved. It could be Druidism; it could be conventional witchcraft; it could be shamanism—even the Native American traditions; the involvement of the trees and animals and stones and elements; these are all very integral to practical magic as it's been observed for at least the last 2500 years.

It doesn't matter what particular flavor of that is explored, so long as it kinda gets the foot into the door into looking into the "greater than" whatever has been agreed to as this common low-level denominator of an agreed upon reality.

Now, we have this basic structure of the "Core of Magick" that you can work off of in your "Magic Schools" from *The Sorcerer's Handbook* and supplement with *Arcanum* and also *Merlyn's Complete Book of Druidism* and any of the texts that are contained in that. And some of the semantics, of course, being not entirely accurate or not entirely up-to-date for the purposes of what we would consider Grade-III or Systemology, but completely valid for the purposes of studying "magick."

Fundamentals of "magick" as a "magical understanding"— as a Grade-I understanding—it's solid. There's no worries about that. However, so... we have whether something's living or not, it has energy; a force that can be changed—it can be manipulated by the will of the "sorcerer," can't cease... well, that there...we have... the point being that everything has energetic potentials; energetic qualities.

We talk about patterns of Cosmic Law; we talk about being able to manifest change in accordance with Will; we talk about being at Cause. But one of the things that should be understood as a "Master" level of understanding is the energy is not just being found in all things and it's everywhere around us...and the potentials and so on... the magician, the sorcerer, the Self—I AM—okay? *That*...the Alpha-Spirit is the one *always* generating the energy for its experience of reality. Make no mistake about that at *any* grade. Okay?

The mental image of being in *this* room; the processing of waves of sound... now, hitting receptors inside of your body, which are used as *"vias."* You know, we say, "Oh, well, a being is inhabiting a point of view of the body and therefore, you know, we're looking out into this universe" and so forth... well, not directly.

The Alpha-Spirit is using the body as a *via*, as a catalyst, as a medium—a channel of communication—which has its own control centers, its "Mind-System," it's connected to a genetic reactive emotional and biochemical system, and then the actual physical body that is applying "force"—any kind of physical effort—in the universe, at the end result of all that.

And that result, by the way—if you haven't noticed—when we speak of "Prime Thought" or "Alpha Though" and then "Will" interacting with the "Mind System" of the Human Condition; and the intricacies of the "Mind-System" and the reactive and emotional systems and the biochemical... we're describing the Standard Model of Systemology. I mean, it was a logical progression—that Standard Model didn't just develop from nowhere. Of course.

So this is important to know—because whether you are presenting the Standard Model of Systemology in your "Magic Course" or not, the principles behind this... that is why we say: at a higher level of understanding, we just sit there and go "Bop! Bop! Bop! This is what's taking place." It's really easy to understand; real easy to chart.

The reason we needed to understand this is because obviously we run into certain invalidations and criticisms that have affected our mental systems—the Mind-System. It would be one thing to say that, you know, a highly actualized person that can just direct their Will and be at this serene sense of Beingness and occupy a physical form at Will and go out to other universes...okay, but, to break out of the point of view of being in the physical body, in the physical condition, we have to elevate an Actualized Awareness and begin to break agreements that we have conditioned that our point of view and our considerations of reality are confined to this existence.

This can't be done overnight... it *could* be, but it in all likelihood, it's worked at at a gradient scale. Because if you shoot too high and miss, chances are—I mean, some people can just continue applying the same effort; that would be a highly actualized thing to do: not be affected by missing a point and apply the same effort the next time as if it had never even happened. That's what we call perfect duplication. That's a highly actualized ability—but what generally is the case, is that as one reaches and falls short, the willingness and the effort applied, any kind of interest even in doing that, it becomes less and less.

What "magic" *is* very useful for, is beginning to break certain patterns and cycles of thought; patterns and cycles of behavior. Whether or not these means are the *best* and most effective to reach the *highest* levels of Actualization and command of the Mind-Body communication connections and so forth... well... we've come up with better since then, but some of it seems kind of "high" to reach at, and one of the ways which we've found, and most of the people in this room, a lot of our members, their first steps were really into this *Pathway* had to do with what we consider Grade-I or Grade-II work. They didn't just go from life and their lifestyles being what they were and suddenly happen upon Systemology out of the blue and suddenly, go "well, this is great."

Most of them have worked up out of other "New Age" systems; most of them have had backgrounds with other "New Age" systems, mystical traditions, spiritual paths, religions... [*laughs*] "psychology educations"... and this had led us to *now*. And really on that which was worth carrying with; only that which holds up—holds water, sustains the test of time, the acid-test of truth and all these things... only that which was carried with... could be said to be valid for our Systemology.

So, it *does* become more and more refined as we work up, *but* it doesn't become more rigid or confined or fixed to a certain parameter; it becomes more refined in terms of a better understanding—wider understanding—of what has later been chopped into countless fragments and traditions and paths and versions, of which we haven't gotten much closer to those fundamental truths when only occupying *those* point of views. There may be better point of views than being stuck in the most rigid and lowest considerations of the Human Condition.

But, it's not up and out... we're not all the way through... And as I mentioned yesterday—we have seen countless individuals that have traversed what has *felt* or been a *version of* all "seven" or "seven-plus-one" paths, gates, levels, degrees of actualization—but all still within that first level. And so, I mean—we don't really need to systematize it out that way. But if you were to consider that there are seven main levels, gates or divisions, gradients, up to, you know, our Infinity on our model... and each has seven... well, that would be forty-nine, plus the Earth one, that would be Fifty Gates or fifty divisions between *here* and Infinity—or what we art treating as "Source" for at least *our* comprehension of Alpha existence at this point. We may get to that point and find out that there's even much more, because of course, Infinity is Infinity.

We've spent so much time... as a being... on this *Pathway*... as an Alpha-Spirit descending to this point—so much time looking away from the point of Nothingness, the Absolute, the Infinity of Nothingness that we represent as "8" or the Infinity on the Standard Model. We fix the Alpha-Spirit at "7" and then corresponding from that, since we've discussed it already today, we have "Alpha Thought" or "Prime Thought" at "6," with "Will" at "5."

The entrance of the "Mind-System"—what we call the "Master Control Center" in Systemology—at "4," including beta-thought through "3" down to the "Reactive Control Center" of the genetic vehicle at "2" and its emotional levels and degrees all the way to down through "1" to zero, the continuity "mass" of the physical universe. At "zero," I mean, that would be like a "dead body," when all mass is basically the same, the inert physical mass of material existence.

That's the Standard Model.

And we've been able to use that quite effectively in Systemology—and we can use it quite effectively to have a masterful understanding and use of traditional magic. But, the point being: is that at "7" the Alpha-Spirit has spent so much of its existence looking "downward"; looking towards a "something" as opposed to turning around and looking at the "Nothing"—at the Infinity of Nothingness.

So, we've simply plotted the Alpha-Spirit at "7" and then of course, this other point or gradient as Infinity properly so, with the sidewards "8" being "Infinity." But, until we get to those vistas; until we become Actualized as Alpha-Spirits on this gradient path, it's virtually impossible to ascertain *what* Infinity is. Therein lying one of the pitfalls of all of the religious and that kind of traditional...because we got a lot of issues.. well, we don't have a lot of issues... a lot of issues were presented *to* us—people *had* issues—with us presenting Mardukite Zuism in a "religious" sense.

Mesopotamian Neopaganism...why not? Why shouldn't it be represented amongst Druidry and Celtic and Norse Wicca and all these other practices? Presenting it as a religious framework... these people also seem to forget that Wicca and Druidry are also presented as a religious framework, I guess...

These practices in the past have had a tendency to define Infinity, you know, as being the "God" point for our purposes on the standard model, without barely even being able to actualize the Individual at the other end of the spectrum. When we look at the "Spheres of Existences" one-through-eight as they apply: you know, one being Self; eight being that Infinity or that Source; seven being Spirit... they seem to have a lot of certainty and impose a lot of morals and dogmas concerning truths about that, without having any understanding of Spirit, any understanding of the Mind, and very little understanding of the reactivity and control centers of the Human Condition, which are an interactive point.

The reason we study the Zu-line or the Standard Model or these higher, just, you know, intellectual points of this Systemology, is to have a better understanding of what is taking place as reality, as existence: life, universe, everything. Because when we look at the model we see that the point between Alpha spiritual existence (that which is outside this universe) and Beta existence, is the "Mind-System." And right above that, we have "Will."

So what we're talking about is using "Will," this Alpha sense, this direction of Alpha intention, *in* beta-existence. And that would be all fine and good with a nice clear pathway, but you see here, we got "Will" going into the Mind-System. So, now we've got the confounded turbulence and aberration and fragmentation and all of this happening here in the Mind-System, which is connected here to this emotional reactive system, where things like pain and unconsciousness and loss and memories of this type of stuff all begin to inhibit and affect what we're willing to do; how we're willing to perceive things.

That's why I say: what's happening out there, there's masses out there that are being given significance; that are being created for your mental imagery in your Mind and in your Mind's Eye—this is all happening by Self. And so when we start to deal with the energy and bringing energy as a fundamental before throwing a bunch of rituals and spells and incantations at someone in a "Magic School"—it's just important that they really get this down as a premise.

So the reason we bring this up is because the Standard Model could be just as easily applied to an understanding of magic and what's taking place with magic and also ensuring that a Seeker understands what they're going to be getting out of it. When we're talking about Will interacting with the Mind-System, an individual is willing something into being and yet at the same time, that energy has to pass through all of their mental stuff and all of their emotional stuff in order to make a demonstration out in the physical existence.

This becomes—this is one of the reasons why we've actually expressed, even though we've removed a lot of the esoteric qualities out of Systemology and tried to make it a little bit more of a fundamental universalist Self-Help Ascension path, these fundamentals apply all across the board and we have even suggested that it actually improves your ability to practice magic, because your understanding... all of the limitation and intricacies of what is taking place in the Mind-System. You're trying to use the Mind to affect change; you're trying to use the Mind to have a command of Self and its conductance of energy with other energies that you are interacting with in the physical existence—why isn't it always working?

And when people have found too many invalidations along this path, they usually quit; they turn around and go back the other way—they go back to the point that seemed to work for them most and they cling to that, and usually never rise into other gradients. So, although we're not introducing (Grade-III) "processing" at Grade-I, systematic processing as we teach at higher grades, it's still important that an individual is at least aware of that they are carrying around a lot of mental and emotional stuff that *will* get in the way of them applying "Will" from an Alpha point into affecting changes in beta-existence.

Now, we've found in rituals that this has been described in various ways, but mostly with the "creation of a circle." An individual is creating a (ritual) circle and the best that we've been able to use semantically with Grade-I and level-one in magic in semantics and even the sciences, is "microcosm."

They say, "well, I'm creating this little circle here and this is my space; this is my version of the material universe." And then they begin to conduct and, various actions and movements with various significances that are all ascribed to it—and that is essentially "uploaded" into what they consider their agreement or their reality and their later experiences with the physical existence.

But there is actually something much deeper taking place here and this is something we treat, again, at higher Systemological levels—but that's important for a Grade-III Master understanding of all this: is that we're not just creating a microcosm of the physical universe—that would be *agreeing* to all of the parameters and sets of the physical universe *as* its experienced at this lowest common denominator.

We know that Cosmic Law is actually—although it only governs the physical existence; beta universe—we know that Cosmic Law is not the fullest extent to which things operate. We also know that most individuals carrying the Human Condition aren't even remotely aware of Cosmic Law and how it all operates; they aren't even able to use these higher laws as they apply to the physical universe and get the results that they want *down here.*

So, this application of "creating separate space" *is* a "practice"—a practice for the individual as Self, while still occupying the point of view of operating as physical bodies —of creating a personal universe; creating space. Space... it's assumed that "space" is always just *there*; space is just everything that's out there... but, all of this is interacted with as points of Awareness. Awareness has to be given; and suddenly there is an interaction—there is something there to be interacted with; a person then has an experience.

Everything else is strictly "mental images." And even when we're interacting with what we see before us, the very fact that we are seeing it in any respect, it is going through how many different control centers and wires and channels to give us that information; all of which are only as clear as the channels that they are being sent on. And this is one of the things that is emphasized more in the direct methods of "processing" that we introduce in Grade-III, because a lot of Seekers up until this point have not necessarily reached these vistas automatically or as a guarantee by following these rigid lower-grade systems of magical understanding.

And understand that we are only working backwards this way; the magical understanding that we're exploring in Grade-I, at best, covers what we can account for over the last 2500 years—and everything prior to that we treat in Grade-II as Mesopotamia, where even then, our paradigm and our worldview and the perspective shifts within that wider encompassing understanding, at which point we flip back up in Grade-III and look at where all this is going to.

So, we're taking a close look at the immediate present and immediate past, the distant past and then now, the present that we're actually at and then the future. And by that point, with a Mastery of all that—all that understanding—then we definitely have someone worthy of the title of "Master."

The other point here that I must express, because it's given in the very first paragraph of the *Sorcerer's Handbook*—and which again, we have a better understanding of certain things now as they pertain to the physical universe, as they pertain to the study of magic—these things are still valid for the study and practice of magic.

But, unfortunately, within the practice of "magick" and what the magician is actually trying to escape or break the gravity of, is this concept of "conservation of energy," which has been instilled within the physical universe. This "conservation of energy" basically firmly states that "energy cannot cease to exist, nor can it be created, it simply is."

So, we're sitting there looking at this material universe that at this level of understanding has basically still been created *for* us; we're kind of only blind participants in; and it is still very much agreeing to this idea of the "conservation of energy," which basically—that is to say that the universe is designed to persist and only to persist and basically just remain solid.

If nothing can be created or destroyed, according to it... See? That's where the individual comes in and this is where we start to see the difference between being at "Cause" and being the "Effect." Being at the "effect" is basically a whole hundred percent agreement with the efforts of the physical universe against the individual as Will and as a Spiritual being existed in it. And if you were actually one hundred percent in agreement with the forces of the physical universe, your point of view would be occupying a dead body...or a rock... very fixed and no real movement to speak of.

Obviously we can actually chart that that's the direction that humanity is going in; and unfortunately, even the practice of traditional "magick" as it's been done—see this is why things have degraded. If the information, the knowledge and the message and the communications had been perfectly duplicated over these 6000 years since the foundation of the Ancient Mystery School, we wouldn't have this degradation of knowledge and this sparse fragmented understanding of which has basically led us only into further trappings of the material universe.

And that's why I said previously: a lot of these magical systems *are* spiritual traps *if* they are treated as the end-all be-all. Because so long as you are still dealing with the domains of working with the material universe; trying to get by just a little bit better in the material universe; you're using "spells" and "rituals" and creative visualization to basically only reinforce the solid reactivity that you already have— you have solid reactivity about love and lust and wealth and greed and all these things; well, geez, if you just supercharge that a little bit more, by all means you're gonna get stuck further and further into the Human Condition.

Well, lookee there: for those that were able to break free of the gravity and see that there's just something a little bit "more" out there in which to hold onto—in which to grab in which to get out of—well, it just sends you right back, because all you've done is made your reactivity, your programming and your imprints, that much more solid for both this lifetime and potentially thereafter.

For that reason, we are working to develop the Mardukite Master Course from a point of Self-Honesty and examine these systems and traditions for exactly what they are—and for heaven sakes, don't get stuck in them.

: LECTURE 7—A HISTORY OF MAGIC :
(September 22, 2020)

History seems to run pretty parallel with the study and practice of "magick." So, a history of magic and a history of the development of (the) Human Condition—human civilization—pretty much run parallel. You can pretty much guarantee to be running into one when you are pursuing the other—pursuing the nature and basis of these various traditions and how they developed; how they relate to one another—you are basically dealing with the *history* of these traditions.

Now, it's very possible to present a introductory class on the "History of Magic" and, you know—if we are going to consider a "Magic School" and examples, you might have even heard of, for example, from "Harry Potter" and so on and so forth—we talk a lot about the "History of Magic."

I personally—I've never written a discourse exclusively on the "History of Magic" or just "history" in general. It's always been an integrated study into whatever tradition or system that I was working on describing. Now, you can do intro classes based on "magick," you could do intro classes that, you know, pertain to "basic tech" and "ritual tech."

Though a lot of times a "History of Magic" is a simple starting point, or an orientation concerning all of the traditions. Now, if you're running someone through the structure of, for example, Grade-I Route-A and dealing with the *Sorcerer's Handbook* and its descriptions of the various traditions, you are going to run into history all throughout that, because as you start to get into the "spell and ritual" traditions that were mostly propagated by, for example, the "witchcraft" traditions, and you start to deal with the history of "Wicca."

If you start to look too far behind "elemental magick" and the "Druidic" traditions, well, it begs the question of "who the Druids are." And of course, when you get into the more traditional origins of "ceremonial magick" and some of the practices that predate the founding of "Wicca" in the early 1900's, then you're dealing with the Golden Dawn; you're dealing with the Rosicrucians, Aurum Solis, and various traditions that each represent the history of, at least, "modern magick" or at least the modern—well, as it was described in the late 1800's (as the) "magical revival."

This "magical revival" (quote; unquote) has been going on for almost 150 years.

When I was developing the *Sorcerer's Handbook* and a lot of the original Grade-I material, this would have been in the late 1990's. When I was working with the "Elven Fellowship Circle of Magick" in Denver, that was between like '98 and 2000. The work for the *Druid's Handbook* was done by 2001; most of the *Elven* work—the *Elvenomicon*, *Book of Elven-Faerie* —was done by 2004. And *Arcanum* was being developed between 2006 and 2008.

Most of this goes back to what was inherently a part of the late-1990's "magickal revival" which was pretty much like an apex for the "New Age" just as it had been many generations prior, with the early figures and the rise of exposure concerning "magick" in Western Europe—the late 1800's; early 1900's.

So really we have been coming up to speed when considering the "New Age" literature and where things kind of reached as a pinnacle point in the late 1990's—before the 21st century. Really, the 20th century was bringing to light a lot of the "mysterious" and "esoteric" and "occult" traditions that originally, if you weren't... if you didn't know someone, if you weren't initiated, if you weren't coming to, for example, a "magick class" or a "Master Course" such as this—if you weren't directly involved through some underground network or channel, you didn't really have access to this material; the kind of materials that are thrown around so easily now.

And that is what actually makes—defines—this point that we reached in the late 1990's when everything could be laid out. When we look at the history and development of what's available as a Grade-I study, in the materials as they were presented *when* they were presented—they are just as relevant then as now. Some biographical information has been updated; for example, in *Arcanum* concerning different individuals in there: changes and deaths and so forth.

But really, we haven't seen—other than the work of the Mardukites, which is one of the reasons why I developed this foundation in 2008 and pushed through to 2009 until it was a solid research organization—there really hasn't been much of note; and so there really hasn't been any reason to validate; just because the internet has become what it is today—there's obviously a greater population on the planet; more people interested in this as a demographic; many groups and circles and would-be independent authors and so forth, are all, you know, come and gone or still...

I have no reason to validate any of that or make any of that a part of the traditional "History of Magic" or with the "Master Course" or what we are doing, because very little of it really runs synchronous with what we are trying to do and our efforts to pushing to higher points... Grade-I material is as it stands. "Magick" and the mysticism; the "Dragon" tradition throughout thousands of years; the "Druids" —this is all as it stands.

What's been carried forth from that—other than some aspects of archaeology or whatever new sciences might validate—it's been established. And all we've really seen in the 21st century is a "watered-down" version of what we were trying to reach from the underground occult scene in the 1990's; something I was an integral part of, operating as

"Merlyn Stone" and with the *Draconomicon*, the *Sorcerer's Handbook*, and some of the other underground work at that time.

But now, everything's changed and has become kinda this convoluted mess; most of which has, as I was describing previously (in a former lecture), only solidified further and further restraints, restrictions, parameters and paradigms *of* a Grade-I understanding, with really no assumption of anything "greater."

The few that do delve into what would fall under Grade-II work and some of the higher "Hermetic" mysteries as they were relayed, usually still fall short of finding any practicality with that; it's usually always brought back to a Grade-I level, ceremonial magic and so forth.

When we look at the *history*, you can definitely—you could apply just the historical aspects as I've described them, either through the *Arcanum* material or pulling out the historical aspects from *Merlyn's Complete Book of Druidism*, the *Draconomicon*, the *Elvenomicon*, the *Druid's Handbook*... and Grade-II is... concerning the Ancient Near East, Mesopotamia, Babylon... plenty of "history."

An individual could spend the rest of their lifetime focused exclusively on the "History and Development of Magic." If you throw in "theory" with that—you could still occupy someone without ever getting around to any "basic tech" or "ritual tech" concerning "Magick and Mysticism."

One of the reasons why an individual—a Master or such—would put their apprentice through some rigorous studies of just dry "History of Magic" is not only to just orient some framework or pursuit of specific traditions, would be to "weed out" those who are coming to something described as a "Magic Course" strictly for other purposes...with really no interest in getting on a *Pathway to Self-Honesty* and Self-Actualization and achieving "greater than human" heights in terms of Actualized Awareness and pursuing something beyond the Human Condition. They are still quite fixed to it.

The concept of Magic to them might be simply "control"—wanting to "control" others or wanting to simply be more... strengthen, like what we were saying previously in the former lectures—strengthen their own imprinting, their own reactivity, their own programming, rather than using "Magic" as a means *out of* it.

So, using "History of Magic" classes can actually weed out some of those that really are just showing up trying to figure out what the next "spell" would be, and so forth. Now, you're still gonna have to cater to that element concerning Grade-I work, because for some that's really where it's at. And for some that will really be the first practice that they've even had in this lifetime of trying to direct something at Cause or be more at Cause in terms of the energy that they're directing, what they're feeling, their outlook.

Because, keep in mind that, with all magical practices: it is the magician that is changing. It is the magician that is becoming the transmutation...in alchemy. It is not the outer world; it is the fact that the magician—the Self—is always the one projecting their experience *of* that outer world. And it really does boil down to where they are at.

So when we deal with "history" as it pertains to Grade-I, just entry-level Grade-I type work, you're gonna find two real key elements that have appeared in the 1900's after work of the Golden Dawn—now these *were* members *of* the Golden Dawn, so you could work this in two directions. You could work this from the recent history *back* to Mesopotamia. Or, you could work from Mesopotamia *up to* recent history; or you could just pull out all the sections and various elements that describe history to compose a class on the "History of Magic."

Otherwise, the bottom line being that you're going to stick

to the literary tradition as we have described. I believe Samuel Kramer said it best when he said that "history began in Sumer" and by that we mean the "written word"—history as records and actual accounts written from human hands concerning human perspectives of what's taking place or what's happening or what's considered knowledge for any given point in time.

We have about—at best—6000 years of that.

Now, of course, we've uncovered a lot more concerning "Cosmic History" and "past lives" and other "universes" and all kinds of stuff in Systemology—and upper-level Systemology—which is where all of this is kind of leading to.

Once a "Master" has gained a "Mastery" of *this* material universe and then an understanding of the *systems* within this material universe—then we can consider higher points of Awareness, but we don't really jump the gun on that, nor do we want to hold anyone back.

However, giving a "History of Magic"—it's going to come up one way or another. You're either going to be constantly trying to piece it together with what they already know or what's understood; because granted we are not dealing with a subject that's taught in the average public school system or anything of that nature. Aside from some basic geography and perhaps some of the politics governing the *exoteric* or *outer* observations of world history, there is very little point of reference concerning the "magical" traditions and the underground streams that have flown for 6000 years.

For some, just even the "History of Magic" and the exploration that this stuff *has* even taken place *is* part of a breakthrough or an "Awakening" or an "entry-point," because again, it still is already going beyond this common low-level denominator agreement of what is taking place in the universe; or what *has* taken place—for one, where *we* come from: concerning human history and human civilization.

So, we are dealing with something here that is already beginning to *break* the ties that have formed in a conventional study or a conventional understanding of history when we start to look at what's been taking place beneath the scenes.

Many of those who were involved with the modern traditions of "Wicca," *witchcraft* and the "neopaganism" that it spurred and also the "Druidism" and the various factions of that... does link back to the Golden Dawn, the Rosicrucians and the Freemasons and *that* level of work that was taking place in the late 1800's and the early 1900's.

Wicca, for all intents and purposes and as is explored academically and historically, there's really very little basis for it before the 20th century. Most of the traditional witchcraft, Wicca traditions, the explorations into and so forth, really stemmed from the work of Gerald Gardner. And Gerald Gardner was also friends with Aleister Crowley and Ross Nichols (which is a figure that was significant in the development of Druidism). And all of this was taking place in England.

In the early 1900's in America, what we were really seeing was more of a philosophical approach—and the only real "mysticism" that had developed here and was specific *to* America, was "American New Thought." And this was—rather than being imported from the esoteric traditions of Western Europe, was actually a Western synthesis of Eastern thought.

Even in some of the Theosophical aspects—Theosophy being a school and foundation established by Madame Blavatsky in the late 1800's, virtually the same year that the Hermetic Order of the Golden Dawn was founded. And we see these parallels often—two streams that seem to develop around the same time.

We deal in a lot of history again when we start to look at Route-D and the evolution of Druidry in the European tradition. :But even in that revival, we best trace a synchronous revival of not only "neodruidic" practices as a secret society and fraternity, but also English Freemasonry—both simultaneously being established in the year 1717 at a, well virtually a, pub, called the Apple Tree Tavern.

So there again, two unique streams, that again, both established actually in the same geographical point and in the same year. The one, the Druidic arm of that, mainly established by John Toland, who is the author of the *Pantheisticon*, which not only did we release a "tercentenary" three-hundred anniversary of that for the Systemology Society a couple of years back, but it also appears in your *Instructor's Manual* version of the *Master Course* material as a supplement to the Grade-I Route-D material, and in the supplement of *Merlyn's Complete Book of Druidism.* There you go "full-circle" there too.

Now prior to these figures like Gardner and Nichols and Crowley and what not, of the revivals taking place in the 1900's, really one of the few sources that we had prior to that were the works that were being prompted [promoted] by the Golden Dawn and their translations, such as the *Key of Solomon* and *Sacred Book of Magic of Abramelin the Mage.* And it's unique that some of the more ceremonial versions of, like for example, neopaganism, Wicca and witchcraft thereafter—you actually begin to see elements of this encroaching into it, which is why having an understanding of the diverse traditions and its histories is significant.

Because in these supposed grimoires that are derived from the "rural witchcraft" traditions and what they call "FamTrads"—these "family traditions" that supposedly existed for hundreds of years—we find incantations from John Dee's work in "enochian magic" of the 1500's; we find "magic squares" taken from the *Sacred Book of Magic by Abramelin the Mage.*

The "*Golden Bough*" is another great work—Sir James Frazer, he basically began classifying a lot of the traditions and customs of the ancient pagan folk. Again, there's no reason to get incredibly tied into these as a modern practice; or required to be practicing all of these various folk traditions—but it is an interesting study to pursue in terms of how these evolved and how some of the symbolism and traditions *were* preserved in the rural "pagan" and "folk" country traditions during the Christianization of Europe and the eradication of these "pagan" or "magical" traditions on a wide scale.

So that's really where we find the "origins" of "modern magick." The real—the real turning point *being* the late 1800's. I would say, in terms of "modern magick"—now a lot of these grimoires and manuscripts in various languages and pursuits, mostly based on the Hebrew or Semitic "Kabbalah" were emerging all throughout the 'middle ages' and this is mainly a response—again a Western-approach response, or an uninitiated's response—to one of the only streams that was still carrying widely a mystic tradition at the time, which was Jewish Mysticism: the Kabbalah.

Now, we know in studying deeper that the Semitic Kabbalah is *directly related* and *derived* from work of the Babylonians and the "StarGate" system—their "Ladder of Lights," establishment of the division of "Spheres and Circles"—and similarly our Standard Model. But, what ended up resulting was a series, again, of "outer court" "outer level" "outer circle" understandings of deep mysticism—deep traditions—and the systematization of it for purely ritual and ceremonial purposes.

So now you had more "pathworking" and all these various: "well, this now has this color assigned to it, it's this number, it's this pathway, it's assigned with this archangel and this cherub and this demon and devil" and a whole pattern and paradigm of ways in which this was brought to... solidified.

In a previous Mesopotamian tradition, you do see a correspondence between the planetary forces and the Anunnaki deities—you see a bridge between the mythological figures, the deities, the pantheons, those which appear as the main figures in all of the oldest texts and which were the first pantheon of deities for "paganism" to be "worshiped" in our history.

And then you see relays of these various—same patterns—appearing throughout geography and time, across history and into various cultures and each time becoming more and more specific, more and more refined, but also quite different from its original source traditions. And so therein again it's important to see where the history and magical developments lie.

Now, by the time we get into our new Systemology and some of the developments that we drew from Ancient Mesopotamian Tablets—what we call the "Arcane Tablets" or anything that is being used for Systemology—we really expect that a lot of the "mystery" surrounding the history and traditions is going to be *flattened*; that at this juncture we can simply focus on the "energies," the Self, what Self is doing, Alpha and Beta existences, the relay and communications taking place...and so forth; management and control of, not only the Mind-Body connection, but mental image—total absolute command of Self.

Now, that's what we are shooting for. And to reach that point, we have to make sure that the "mystery" and the "glamour" and the "allure" and the Effect of "magick" and these "magical traditions" has been securely *flattened*. So, we want to make sure that at least a broad understanding of this backbone of tradition has been relayed.

Of course, when you get into the origins of witchcraft and Druidry and so forth, you are moving away from the Americas here, and we are going back into Europe and we are getting into, well, where things kinda got pushed to in England and developed there for the Western world; but also, how they reached that point (in England) and that's dealt with exclusively for Route-D and understanding the Druidic tradition.

History will keep cropping up as you move farther and farther back into history and the development of these traditions; and rather than seeing them become more complicated and seeing them develop into more diverse methods and traditions and perspectives on it, we reach the —almost like a zero-point in Mesopotamia—because we see all of the original, at least as they are intended, applied to *this* human civilization; so the human civilization that resulted in the last 6000 years to get us to where we are today.

This says nothing about what has taken place before and other buried continents or anything of that nature—we're referring specifically to what we can trace back with any certainty, what we can find evidences for in museums (if we take the time to), the cultures and traditions that even anthropologists have studied at an academic level (whether or not they have any deeper understanding of what they're looking at)—and so that's one of the reasons why we don't need to impress "if you haven't gone to school for such and such" and "well, you need to have a degree in this to understand this"—we are providing a "Master Course" and Master-level course *in* the applications of practical mysticism, the development of it, its history, all the way back into Mesopotamia... I mean we're talking esoteric archaeology; not even the stuff you're going to find in "history books" necessarily, unless you go looking for these specific details.

At any kind of just "conventional" level of standard, you know, "Ancient History 101"—in most instances, you won't see Mesopotamia dealt with too much with anything that... any textbooks or curriculums that are from the 20th century. There's a little bit of discussion concerning the "cradle of civilization" and Mesopotamia is the two rivers and Hammurabi and... and then it's back to "classical history." So, we have a solution for that; we have Grade-II, which delves into the heart of Mesopotamia and its evolutions and history.

In the course of this we have at least a summary of 6000 years of human history. You can get as far into it as you want. There is a brushing of it in the *Sorcerer's Handbook*; there's also a treatment of each individual aspect of it in *Arcanum*. And you can create a "timeline" if you want—you can create a "timeline" of these developments.

You can (work out) little streams and branches of how they've developed, but primarily you're gonna want to focus on—when you're looking at the Mardukite Master Course— you're gonna want to focus on those elements, again, that might direct an individual toward a higher appreciation and understanding and not necessarily the "New Age" sources that are available today.

For that reason, we've been able to develop *The Great Magickal Arcanum* and this new edition of it as *A Master Course in Magick for Modern Wizards*—this is an incredible feat in just trying to cement and *flatten out* that which an individual is most likely going to be in search for: the little snippets, the little factoids, the rituals, the spells, the correspondences... and put it all in one place, so that they don't need to spend the rest of their—this lifetime—pursuing this information, which is at this juncture, already been laid out into the light.

There's very little at this point—for Grade-I understandings —that an individual would need to join up with a specific organization or correspondence course or some secret society or some...something that would take *more* money, time, resources, energy and Awareness in this lifetime to just reach a master-level of understanding with. And that's something that *we* can provide quite easily using it as a step to move farther along on the *Pathway*.

Now, again, if there's any real interest that a Seeker has, you are going to want to focus on those. One of the things that an Apprentice-and-Master relationship has is *communication*. This requires observing—being actually observant of—your Seeker, of apprentices, and where they're at. And so, an intro class on magic—"The History of Magic"—basic techniques and seeing where a person is at, you'll be able to kind of judge where you need to aim your particular focus in keeping them with, at least, a gradient step of "wins" that will keep them pursuing this and not become disinterested or invalidated.

So, look for the points in history that they may have an attachment to. It's very likely that one of these systems or traditions or semantics or flavors *is* actually "keyed-in" to their programming; something that they may be here in this lifetime trying to resolve—something that is unresolved or something that they participated in, in a former lifetime, which is now within their grasp and reach to be able to be fully *flattened* and be able to move forth.

Because until we get into higher level work and really get a person opened and actualized enough to explore whatever it is they may have done in former existences to bring them to this point—and with the kind of imprinting and beliefs and fragmentation that they have at this point—look for... just, keep your eyes open. Look for these key points that seem to register with them; either some kind of recognition or some kind of reactivity—anything that's an attraction or repulsion, and you should be able to start having a good understanding of where to start aiming the remainder of your (magical) curriculum at, in order to bring them along the *Pathway.*

: LECTURE 8—BASIC MAGIC TECH :
(September 22, 2020)

[Okay, now that we're getting midway into the day here, I want to get some information out there to you concerning "basic tech" and its application in magic—and then we'll go ahead and break for lunch.]

So, we'll call this "Magic Tech"—"Basic Magic Tech." And what are we dealing with? We want to apply "higher level" understandings to the operations of "ritual magic" and so forth. We want to reinforce—as we're moving along here—that we are slowly breaking agreements with the "Physical Universe" as we begin to approach and practice "traditional magick."

A lot of symbolism—in the absence of both knowing and the objects themselves—a lot of diverse symbolism of the *terminals* of energy, and a lot of this—when we start to deal with higher-level gradients of Systemology—we kind of jokingly make a lot of comments concerning the trappings of the "magical traditions" and so forth as we discover them, as they become more apparent.

Other than as an entry-point into higher-level work, it isn't something that we impress as much—something that I would impress as much, as perhaps I would have 15 or 20...25 years ago—it's simply a gradient on which we work forward, mainly because whatever point we're working with, whether it's "ritual magic" or Systemological "processing," we're always dealing with the "*somethings*" as opposed to the "*nothings.*"

And so we have images and pictures, we have names and labels—all of which have associative meaning, which is then given significance. This significance could be in terms of thought, the way we associate the data and its associations with other data, or it could be *emotive*, it could have some sort of sensation or emotion attached to it as a reaction—whether it's attractive or repulsive.

Something's that's being desired, or something that's being kept away, all of that is not overcome within a Grade-I tradition—within this... "magick" as it is given traditionally, which is one of the reasons—why, like I said: I don't really impress it as a primary vehicle of "Ascension." It's just something's that *there*—something that your not gonna get passed (without dealing with).

Virtually all of us have explored some facet of (magic) or another along the way, and so by having a masterful presentation of it, we can be certain that a Seeker isn't going to succumb to these lesser applications.

Now, at any point, these considerations are *all* taken into account concerning an individual—the Alpha-Spirit, the I-AM's—point of reference concerning its own creative ability; its own ability to *do* something. And we find these steps —these same steps—practiced in a "ritual" setting, when we, for example, create sacred space: a *nemeton* or a circle or the square-cube of the room—however, its represented—whether its outdoors or in a temple.

The point being that the act of creating space is the uppermost point of the creative ability of Self, which is *being*. The creation of space is the point of *beingness*—the point of view on which we are extending our reach out into the universe. And when we start to deal with energy—when we start to deal with the energy, the activities, the motions—well, then we're dealing with a *doingness*. We're dealing with actual *activities* that are being observed or directed *from* that point of view within the space that was created.

So, these same steps that we deal with in higher-level "processing"—the "Wizard Grades," creative uses of Systemology—the same principles apply anywhere where older magical traditions and techniques are effective. They're only effective because they somehow work along or correspond with these higher principles that we've been able to establish—that's the only reason that they operate.

Some of them do not necessarily operate for the best optimum success of the individual. They're simply "functional." And that's one of the things that we can recognize. One of them being the mechanistic nature of the programming—remember that, when we're dealing with "magick" and we're dealing with the "material existence" and we're dealing with "beta" universes, we are dealing with the "Mind Systems." We are dealing with an interactive communication point between an upper-level Being and whatever it is set up as channels for communication and interaction at these other levels.

One of the things that happens, is we have "control centers." Control Centers are one example of a mechanistic or patterned *system* that operates at a specific way. This is—this is not necessarily governed directly by Self, this is often times following a specific pattern of function. And so one of the things that we find when we're practicing "conventional magick"—the "tech" of practical magick; "basic magic tech"—we're dealing with *mechanisms*, we're dealing with mental mechanisms and response mechanisms of emotive energy that are all ingrained in the Human Condition.

The magician is not necessarily standing *outside of* the Human Condition... just simply being a Master of it is... but, not necessarily completely *outside* of it. Mastery *is* a point when one shifts one's point of view *outside of*, rather than stuck within, a point of view. However, that's why we have been able to differentiate, for example, the "Master Grades" versus the upper "Wizard Grades."

We're dealing with—at the Master level—with a mastery of the material universe.

One of the ways in which this is communicated—or interacted with—*is* quite specifically these mechanisms which have been set up. And even any of the personal energy systems—anything, if you want to refer to them as "chakras" at this point of development, or any of these control centers—they are all "patterned." They are all "programmed." Not one of which is *actually* "Self," but all of which are *filters* and screens or *vias* or catalysts or channels in which information is being received to formulate the experience that Self is having.

Whether it's operating as an "Actualized Technician" *remote* from the "body," or whether it's the magician seated within this (quote; unquote) "microcosm-universe-space" that they've created, this is what we are working with.

One of the drawbacks is whether or not an individual *is* operating from any degree of Self-Honesty when they begin to apply additional efforts and energies in this work. For example, validating reactive sensations, programming, imagery, as a part of the practice, rather than a resolution of the same. And this is one of the reasons also why some do not find the effectiveness that something is enchanting and whatnot, fantastical as magic actually is, because really what you're running up against is thought-counterthought; you're running against programming that has already been solidified and validated particularly by an agreement to be in a Human Condition or to occupy society at large, you're operating against a lot of programming and conditioned imprints—all of this type of fragmentation—when you begin to practice "magick."

Because you're, again, you're breaking ties—traditional ties—to how the Human Condition is programmed, or the agreements to the programming and the conditions of it, for the Physical Universe as it stands. There is a danger sometimes in just changing programming, but still not understanding or recognizing being at Cause for it.

So, the magician has a tendency to use these ritual settings to basically recondition themselves, but still using a lot of automatic response mechanisms—simply changing the variables or the function that is taking place. Now, in the creation... if we were to treat this specifically as an objective, or something outside of the individual, it's not much different than creating an "elementary being" or some kind of intelligible spirit-lifeforce creation, that you would then send out to conduct some kind of task or to carry some kind of energy or to, just kind of push the "quantum probability" levels of the "sequence of actions" in life in one direction preferably to another.

This is basically what's done when a magician is performing a ritual and then sending out these intentions—and basically establishing these further links and programmed, preprogrammed channels about how they're going to operate. Now, the intelligent thing to do in this respect would be to put some kind of time-frame on it. For one: to be knowingly at Cause in creating and doing this type of activity; and then to put a time-frame on it.

The entity or the energy is to go out and conduct a particular task and then return, or to conduct a particular task and then if a certain amount of time has passed, then to return, or to return to a particular object or return its own energetic universe—things of that nature. These are considerations that should be included in any kind of "magic tech."

Now one of the things that I brought up in one of the previous lectures that we directly confront when dealing with "magick," or any point where the Alpha-Spirit is directing as Cause, is the combination of the two universes. Because what is generally taking place as the Human Spirit has degraded into its present state of the Human Condition and that point of view, is it's been unable to differentiate its own personal universe from the "beta" or "physical" or objective "material" universe.

And so as those considerations of Self become more confined to a body, as considerations of the creative ability of the Spirit has become more confined to the mechanizations of the "Physical Universe," so too does the individual's sense of Self descend to that point.

Really when we take a look at what we're doing with Systemological "processing," even at Grade-III—which falls within the domain of the "Master Course"—we're increasing the ability—particularly the creative ability—of the Alpha-Spirit, because one thing we know is that the Self is consistently *creating* its own personal universe all the time.

We focus more on the "universes" and their creation and management and all of that more at upper-levels, because even to really grasp that, the individual has to come to know—with full realization—that the Alpha-Spirit, they as the Alpha-Spirit, is at cause and creating them. So this comes into direct conflict from, again, what we look at from a purely material physical existence, because again, "conservation of energy"—this idea—is again confining what is possible in the material universe: that this is what is here and that this is what you have to work with and then here are the rules for working with it and most of the time it's simply a copy-and-paste of what's already been done.

And it must be a copy-and-paste a little bit worse, because it's not a perfect duplication; we seem to have lost a lot of knowledge along the way—which we have since reclaimed and recovered, especially at a Systemological level, but not necessarily at the mainstream conventional level.

The individual—the Seeker, the magician—is brought up on a gradient scale to understand that they *can* create and imagine any form; they can create any energy, imagine any form, and that they are the one at Cause to do this. And so when you look at the formulas of "spellcraft"—you look at the way conventional "rituals" work—whether you want to apply a lot of fanciful "witchcraft" semantics to it, or whet-ther you're just looking at it as Self being able to create and manage space and energies and so forth, the various principles remain the same—so long as these other magical traditions don't become the primary focus; that it isn't more about the "symbolism" or *one more* way it can be converted or diverted; that this is still the Self being at Cause, the Self being the creator; doesn't require anything from an outside source.

The most basic "tech" that we have when it comes to "magick" being somehow the "art of visualization"—the art of being able to create and manipulate images in the Mind—is what is referred to as "visualization." And so when you consider the basic formulas of ritual—the "ritual tech"—we have: raising energy; visualizing the change occurring; sending energy to the cause.

And there you have an individual basically *operating* within their own personal universe. Raising energy: meaning basically *creating* the space and then also operating... you're working with the various... What we consider outside energies and whatnot are what we later discover are "*terminals*" and terminals that we ourselves are also creating—because we are creating our experience with them and the significance that they have. Regardless of what they may actually be.

In that being the clincher—that we are able to create and cause the change as to what they are going to be; we are going to create and change an agreement with what they are going to be.

When we sending energy out: a lot of the work that we do in "basic" ritual techniques in any of the Grade-I levels, has a lot to do with the "projection *of*." Later on in Systemology, what we actually find, is that an individual has a tendency to—when they have not reached the state of total Self-Honesty yet—be operating within reactive programming concerning what is attainable and what is not.

In fact, there may be many things that they're implanted to *desire*, which keeps their attentions fixed on such—but which they are also unable to obtain. And so these types of *implanted problems* can sometimes only be further validated when an individual is applying the basic "magic tech" to trying to create these changes. They're simply reinforcing the enforced desires that they have—or the compulsions that they have, or even the repulsions that they have—without actually getting to the source of them, resolving them and reaching a point of knowing and being at cause over them. That none of these have to be the case.

An individual should be completely free and able to consider any of the activities, any of the images—anything—without reactivity.

So, what we end up finding with the "projection" of energy is that an individual has a tendency to "pull" a lot of energies in on *them*. And these energies could be the "mental image pictures"; they could be the images or *themselves*, or any of the imprinted and associated *"charge"* that is attached to memory of the same—and what this does is, if this is (not) treated and only the rituals to try and further satisfy compulsions is being conducted, the individual is not going to be very well off. The "cause" and "point of responsibility" is still displaced.

The individual, rather than taking control of Self, is still waiting for the ritual or the "magick" or the "spell" to create the effects as opposed to Self creating the effect. In doing so, we're still dealing with mechanics of existence; we're still dealing with the universe being at cause—or Cosmic Law being at cause, as it applies to *beta existence*—versus the Self being at cause from an Alpha point, *outside of* the "Physical Universe."

This is one of the reasons why we call this the "Master Course," because if we were simply treating it as I would have in the 1990's—when the *Sorcerer's Handbook* (and *Arcan-*

um) was being developed, even within a purely Druidic framework—we would be treating only the end product of this being that we *can* reinforce and validate existing programming, and therefore keep a person pretty much suspended in the point they're already at—just supercharged with it. And unfortunately, that's just not good enough.

So, we worked much farther along these paths. And we're not going to slight out the individual with "magical" interests because, again, Systemology is so universal and so broad, and approaching a level of truth that—I mean, basically cannot be restricted to any paradigm—that it is sometimes too big of a reach for an individual that is really just coming out of the slumber and slosh of "Awakening" out of a very mundane existence, or one that's just finally reached a certain "flash realization" when the come into contact one of these symbols or flavors or traditions, which they have some sort of link to from the past.

It's important that we are able to, at some point, get a person at "Cause" over, at the very least, their emotional reactivity to *any* of the aspects of the Human Condition that they might later actually be looking to "magick" or some kind of "low magickal spellcraft" or "ritualism" as the solution *for*, rather than the practice of Self-Actualization and the practice of working with energies and the practice of creating space and giving objects significance...all of that gets lost.

So, basically "concentration," "thought discipline"—this is about as far... "grounding techniques"—this is about as far as a conventional Grade-I understanding is going to bring someone. And for those that have difficulties with "mental imagery," this is good practice, up unto the point when this is being dealt with in processing directly—because in "processing" we are dealing with a lot of recall; we're dealing with imagining; we're dealing with scenarios; we're dealing with pulling up mental images that we have reactive-responses to, and dissolving those reactive-responses.

...And to begin being able to free ourselves from the ties that we carry—and the cords and the links and the bonds—that are heavily "*charged*" and which actually keep us secured in this gravitational pull *of* the "Physical Universe."

The magician isn't impervious to that—at this juncture—not at Grade-I. And few are even aware of getting *beyond* the levels of "rituals" and "spells" and relying on other "spirits" or "entities" or "pantheons of deities" to conduct the activities that the Self can knowingly and consciously be doing.

One of the techniques that *is* of extreme benefit—and which does appear in most "magickal primers" but it seems to later fall by the wayside—is the "breathing exercises." One of the reasons why this is of extreme interest—even at a Systemological level—is that the "power of breath," the power to control and regulate the *breathing* of the genetic vehicle—of the physical organism or body—is under the control of Self. Whereas there are many automated mechanisms that we tend to take for granted—and that we can actually control so long as we can first maintain *any* gradient of control over the body; and it usually starts with breathing.

Being able to regulate "breath" also puts one at a *command chair* for regulating the metabolism, regulating the heart rate, regulating the basic emotional state of the genetic organism—because *that's* what we're using as our *via*; that's what we're using as our filter to interact with the "Physical Universe." A lot of times, that seems to be *really* what the individual needs more *of*.

A lot of the candles, spells and incantations and movements are meant to help direct focus—very selectively—and bring a person kind of out of this "mentality" that they're swamped or completely overburdened with human problems that are affixed to the Human Condition.

One of the pretenses to working directly with energy—or rituals, or anything like that, which you *can* employ—would have to do with "breathing." The other thing that comes up in basic magical training is just generalized as "Willpower." And Willpower—at least as we're concerned with the individual, their management of Self, their conductance of rituals, and their experience of the physical universe—really is the entry-point; that's the... "Will" seems to crop up in more "grimoires" and "magick texts" than any other "deity" or "Holy Name" or "mantra."

And so there is basically only a few stumbling points to being able to direct Will *into* the... physical effects—manifestations—and of course we've covered some of those previous today, but the Standard Model (of Systemology) demonstrates it quite clearly, and it's the same Model we use for "processing" and for defragmentation; to be able to clear those channels on which the Will is being able to direct energies and creative ability in the "Physical Universe."

One of the things that gets in the way is generally the compulsions and obsessions and so... an individual—if they want to work up on a gradient scale of Will—anything that they are *compelled* to do, any compulsions, anything that they can't help but do... and can't stop doing—or anything that they can't *start* doing... really falls under that category.

We deal (with) a lot of that in "processing" and some of the "objective" methods in Grade-III and Grade-IV, with the ability to *control* the actions of the body; the ability to control the mechanisms and reactive-responses by controlling the ability to *start* or *stop* various compulsions.

An individual that can't help but do something—get them to do it and get them to do it consciously; get them to know they're doing it and then get them to know to stop doing it and then get them to consciously to start doing it and... *alternate!* We deal a lot with *alternation* of "flows" and "circuits" in processing because it proves to be effective.

For example: the direction and projection of energies—the mental images and the creative pictures—that are practiced in ritual magic, well, we send these away from us and we attract them (into) us; and we refer to them often as "Rays of Light" or we deal with *colors*... or we'll apply whatever the purpose might be, we might apply certain correspondences, whether they're herbs or candles or altar dressings; the colors that we're wearing; the incense that's being burned—anything that gets the attentions directed and focused on control and management of "mental images."

And then, what do we do with them?

Well... you get the individual to basically—perfectly—work with these mental images and visualize them in the ritual setting, with... *knowingly*—knowingly creating them, working with them, making them more solid, and then projecting them, sending them away... and then also bringing them *in*. Projecting away; pushing them in; projecting them away... this is what you're doing in "ritual magic" and this is how you're directing energy in "ritual magic" and this is the *only* element *of* the most basic fundamentals that you're going to find effective.

There's no reason why you can't also incorporate the magical days of the week and "planetary hours" and the phases of the moon and all of these other attributes to your work—if they all contribute to focusing and concentrating the intentions *and* attentions of the individual. Just make certain that the individual—the Seeker—knows that *they are* the one at "Cause" *creating* the imagery; creating the energy; managing the energy—and being able to disperse it at will; having no need to cling onto it.

If you notice: most of the spells and rituals you see—afterward, they refer to you, you know, doing something else. Conducting the ritual; being very intensive, very focused, very concentrated—and then just letting it go, not holding it in, not need... bringing it close. Letting energy run its course. You'll find an individual gets along a lot better the more fluid and the more freely they are able to move, able to act, able to think and do and create.

The more rigid—and solid—these images; anything that's "*charged*," or anything that an individual *truly* has no "control" over, these are the things that end up being *pulled in*, these are the things they end up attracting. And so "ritual magic" and "basic magic tech" is simply a method of *undoing* the nature and polarity of what's being *pulled in* versus what is being "sent out" and the fluidity of being able to direct both at "Cause"—without holding on to tightly and without pushing anything away.

If you practice this as an element of "basic ritual magic"—"basic techniques"—as found throughout *Sorcerer's Handbook* and *Arcanum*, I think you will find the results to be far more effective.

: LECTURE 9—MAGICAL TRAINING :
(September 22, 2020)

[*Okay, welcome back to the afternoon lectures for September 22nd —and before the meal break here, we were talking about "basic magic tech" and introducing magic; concepts of "magick"; "magical schools" and magical training. We got one new person—I guess you can get your notes from a neighbor, or something, until we can get the transcripts...*]

So, what we're looking at here is basically a transition point between Route-A and Route-D... we're scheduled to be on to Route-D by the end of the day here—still within Grade-I. And one of the transition points: that would be "elemental magic"; when you're dealing with "elemental magic"—the elements, natural philosophy—you are dealing with a bridge between Route-A and Route-D; between the *Great Magickal Arcanum* and *Merlyn's Complete Book of Druidism*, or between "Magick and Mysticism" and the "Route of Druidism" within our "Magic School."

One of your points there of commonality is going to be "elemental magic"; and the elements—the *four*, *five* elements— the structure of the universe; the elemental universe. So, people have said that its the structure of the "magical universe." But, the "Magical Universe" is, as we know, basically a universal plane that is referred to in the mystical tradition sometimes as the "Otherworld," the "Faerieland"—in the "high magickal" traditions they deal with some alternate dimensions: "aethrys"...

These are basically alternate form(s) of *beta-existence*—and we don't want to superimpose too much of what we understand as the "occult" or as the structure of the physical universe or our observation of natural philosophy, and superimpose it onto what is actually the "Magical Universe" or "Magic Kingdom," which is, in Systemology—in high-level Systemology—it is the universe we are basically moving ourselves into, as opposed to succumbing to lower and lower fragmentation of *this* universe; we are going in the other direction.

We don't deal too much with that in Grade-I, but when you are dealing with the structure of the universe—you're dealing with elemental magic—you're going to run into the structure of not only the "Physical Universe," but you're going to run into how the "elemental planes" and other perceptions of the "higher" existences are being structured.

These are all structured within specific "kabbalahs," within specific "paradigms," within specific "models" all throughout various philosophies, various paradigms, and ceremonial magic—and in doing that, you can demonstrate that these are (as far as the Magic School is concerned), you can demonstrate that these are the ways that they've been set down in these certain traditions.

However, the sooner—if, you know, get familiar with our... we'll deal with in later lectures... the Standard Model of Systemology—but the sooner you can integrate that into your magical training and magical curriculum, the better; the better for your Seeker. That's not to replace giving them a Master-level understanding of what each paradigm has structured the universes as, or structured their own kabbalah, and their own cosmologies and their own models of...

But, again, we don't want to just leave them hanging in this Grade-I understanding. There's much deeper and higher levels of understanding when it comes to the structure of the universes, the structure of existence, the cosmology of existence—as we have discovered at the Master-Grade or Grade-III level of Systemology, which is all inclusive within the "*Mardukite Master Course.*"

Well I didn't actually prepare notes on this specific delivery of a "Magical Curriculum" from start to finish. Really, most of you—everyone here—probably those even that are going to be getting these recordings even later; you know, you look through *Great Magickal Arcanum*, it's a pretty straightforward arrangement of material. Also, I mean, some... the one's here present... you've all basically been working with this material for almost a decade—and even prior to that, "magical traditions" and other areas.

My purpose is not in relaying it, as I was saying yesterday, in recording an audio-book of all the materials for the Master Course because this is stuff that you can actually read and work through and set up your curriculums on your own. We're not trying to... Of course, at a Master-level, I mean, we are the "Mardukite Academy of Systemology"; we are dealing with Systemology from a Grade-III perspective for the Master Course; we're now working on Systemology at Grade levels IV (*four*) and V (*five*) within the offices apart from this, currently, and have additional grades scheduled beyond that: the sevenfold methodology—the *seven-plus-one* methodology—of the standard Gates.

Now, the point is not to necessarily push your Seekers, you know, to just get them through the grades to a higher level understanding, or to Grade-III to be Masters; that's not necessarily the point of the Master Course. Of course, in delivering the "*Master Course*" we're not just focused on specific grades. I'm delivering this to "instructors" to "Master-level Seekers"—Grade-III level Seekers—that are working through the entirely Master-level of materials that have been released over the past twenty-five years. So, that's what we're doing now.

I'm synthesizing, after twenty-five years of working through this, the "nitty-gritty," so that people can get the most success and the most effective results and move through it. And that's not to say that "magick" is not effective at its own level—within its own paradigms. However, the reason "magick" *is* successful—and this is something we were talking about earlier; I was talking to someone last night about this actually—and we've kind of discussed this in previous lectures now already: that it goes back to the arts of "visualization," you know... I read it first, I think it's coined as coming from Israel Regardie in Douglas Monroe's "*21 Lessons of Merlyn*" but it's: "Visualization is the key to the occult." So, that being the case—we're dealing with "mental imagery," "visualization"... The Mind—and primarily the "nitty gritty" of this being thought: we're dealing with *thought*.

Anything that pertains to *thought* is really all that is effective in "magick" and all that you're really carrying with you to, like, Grade-II and Grade-III; that's basically *it*. All the rest of it is mostly *fluff*. And so—and even at Grade-II—we're dealing with "cultural paradigms," a "magic paradigm," a... basically the "root" mythology behind all existence, so we're dealing with *that* at Grade-II.

But before even that, the real combination here, between Route-A and Route-D is going to be "elemental magic." Now, we're dealing natural philosophy at the point of that—and natural philosophy was once an incredible field of study; natural philosophy was the original... the knowledge of the "priests" and knowledge of the "priestesses"... the ability to *know* things; the ability to observe the universe—to understand anything about the "Physical Universe."

Of course, the greater it became structured and solidified as a material science, the more rigid we became fixed in our considerations about the material universe—the "Physical Universe." So, natural philosophy was still once a great *fluid* observation and *experience* of the natural world. Each time a facet of natural philosophy became overly structured and rigidly agreed to—as a fixed point of view within beta-existence, or the "Physical Universe"—these became "sciences."

And so now "natural philosophy" is pretty much null and... it no longer exists as a main field within our modern civilization; it doesn't really have a place. About the only place it has a place is in the field of "metaphysics" and "mysticism" and so forth, which is usually what brings most of the people here. That's kind of the bottom line behind all this. But at the time it still was a philosophy—and a certain points treated as "religion."

Now, when you look at the "Celtic Druids," it's really a very rigid and fixed and limited perspective to treat it *only* as "religion." If you look up "Druidry"—or "druids"—in the dictionary or encyclopedia, you're going to see that they were the "priests or priestesses of the Celtic people in charge of the Celtic religion."

That's kind of a... when you really look at the core of Druidism and then also the actual history of the Celtic people, that's a vast generalization and oversimplification, because honestly, the Celts in general—the European tribal Celts in general—were very loosely systematized (at best). In fact their systematization was exclusively the Druids and in the charge of the Druids.

For the most part, it was really like two sets of people: you had the *Druids* and the *Celts*. And the Druids may be a part of Celtic society and Celtic history and certainly inspired a lot of the figures and the stories behind the Celtic tradition and mythology. They're really two separate things.

So, let's see... We have "magical curriculum"... So, okay, in *Sorcerer's Handbook*, you are going to find that I really already was pointing towards a higher Systemology—especially, so when this new version... and we're really pleased to see this 21st anniversary collector's edition of *The Sorcerer's Handbook*, this is the first time it's ever appeared in hardcover. And we were able to use some of the old notebooks and manuscripts to attach an appendix to it called the *Lost Books of Merlyn Stone*. And at the very end of it, there was work that I was involved within in 1999, it's called the *Crystalline Sphere* or *Crystalline Awakening*. And this is when I was working with the "Elven Fellowship Circle of Magick."

I was also frequently giving lectures at my high school. I was a junior in high school in 1999, and one of the things that I was frequently doing was giving lectures to particular classes. The two classes that I was involved in: "Mythology" and "Psychology." And so, you know, I've been honestly doing this for over twenty years; that's why we're setting this down as the "Master Course" and recording and probably eventually a volume of transcripts to match your "Instructor's Manual" there, because, you know, this has been set out, set forth, set down, and there's no reason for me to keep going over it again as I move further on.

As the saying goes—[*laughs*] and I won't say who I'm coining this from—as the saying goes, you know, "I'm no longer researching *south*." So, at this point, I'm really only interested in moving the Mardukite Academy into higher levels of training beyond Grade-III and then, of course, the ongoing work that's taking place with Systemology, which is just beyond incredible.

But, of course, we're using the Mardukite Academy and Mardukite Zuism—we're using these as bridges or beacons or gateways, whereas people... "entry-points" onto the *Pathway of Self-Honesty* and getting people into Systemology; getting people in the door.

Given that Systemology itself is really a universalist and spiritual perspective, as opposed to a rigid cultural one... I, of course, went back to Mesopotamia—which we will of course cover in Grade-II—for "Mardukite Zuism" to give a *religious* paradigm, so that, for example, those that are coming in from "magical" or "druidic" or whatever perspectives —the most common, the most level or common ground for this would be "Mesopotamian Neopaganism," which of course has really seen no representation in the modern "New Age."

For all the things that have been revived in the name of "neopaganism" and different brands of "Wicca" and what have you... so what we did with the Mardukites... after a decade of just treating it almost purely intellectually and esoterically as a bridge to higher levels that we're now dealing with in Systemology, we figured that at the... the oldest, the most *basic* paradigm that we can use as a structure, if you want to call it like a quasi-religion, or anything that's going to have any substance in terms of history and traditional mythology, the *backbone* behind the classical—the Greek, the Roman, the planetary-based Celestial Mythologies—we treat Mesopotamia. It just makes sense.

There's no reason for us as being what we are—Systemology or even the Mardukite Academy—to represent any newer or more recent, and of course more fragmented, perspective in that. So, as a cultural religion or mythology or... Mardukite Zuism, we've settled on Mesopotamia, which we will deal more with in Grade-II.

In *Crystalline Awakening*, there's—and parts of this is also in the *"Master Course"* appendix for *Great Magickal Arcanum*—there's various initiations and so forth that we were using at the time. When I worked with the "Elven Fellowship," that kind of sorted to simmer down in 1999, at which point I was kind of putting my emphasis on this other organization that it was evolving into, called "The Hermetic Order of the Crystal Dawn."

The "Crystal Dawn" was meant to really push into what is now being treated as Systemology—the handbook of which I was finally able to release as *"Crystal Clear"* at the end of 2019—and so, we were pushing it at the end there (and this is actually in your *Sorcerer's Handbook*) with various aspects and entire concepts... thinking... where, for example, the "Law of the Mind" when we talk about: Shakespeare says—in *Hamlet* actually—that "Nothing is good or bad except that thinking makes it so."

I'm trying to push people towards *thought* and "The Mind"—and the considerations of such. For example, Buddha saying: "All we are is the result of what we've thought." And other philosophers saying, you know, "Our life is as thought has made it" and "Action follows thought"—and this is basically boiled down to the "Law of the Mind" and that is essentially that: "we are as we think we are" to the extent that we can *Will* ourselves to *Be*.

Unfortunately, this has been so watered-down with modern "New Thought." Modern "New Thought"—the "Law of Attraction," "The Secret"—and all these various things that seem to be very promising, but fail to deliver because of the lack of the "Master-level" understanding, again!—Things we have actually repaired in our Systemology.

If you've seen or dealt with any of these things in the past, you know, and then you look at what we're dealing with in *Tablets of Destiny* or *Crystal Clear*—which is in your "*Systemology Handbook*" (the Master Edition for Grade-III)—we've repaired the watered-down cliché, you know, "positive affirmation"-type elements of, what I would say, the "rise" of quasi-"New Thought, Self Help"-type movement that sort of became popular in the 1970's.

You'll see "Reward Books" and "Parker"... there's a few different old publishers at the time (1970's) that were putting out these "metaphysical occult" books as, like, "professional Self-Help," "business Self-Help," you know, "empower your life" stuff. Honestly, if you look at the state of the world today, obviously most of this is not as... perhaps has helped a few individuals who were more actualized to begin with when they went into even looking at, or trying to understand, these things.

Certainly, if... as much of this material and as much of these "magical traditions" and the "New Age" and all of this "Self-Help" work that's been kind of "mainstream" was actually being as effective as it proposed to be, we should be seeing a different state of things out there than what is taking place. And that's not the case, so...

Obviously there was work to be done—and so that's something that is definitely taken care of... by the time you see the Grade-III work, we're definitely resolving; we have resolved the "New Age," the "magick" and metaphysics, the Druidry, the European Western Magical Tradition, all the way back to basically the origins of *writing*, the origins of history as we know it—the origins of what you can actually see and demonstrate from a historical perspective or what's found in the museums, museum artifacts.

Really, the point being that if we couldn't have effectively demonstrated where this could move further, where this could elevate an individual, where this could actually *evolve* the state of the Human Condition into a new consciousness level, which we are calling *Homo Novus* or *metahuman*, then it didn't mean anything. So after... yeah, after twenty-five years dealing with the occult and metaphysics in *this* lifetime officially, writing about it and all of which—basically since *Draconomicon* in 1995—it's pretty much been set down, it's been established... there's records.

The thing that is going to carry your forth has to do with *thought* and "The Mind." It's true that humans actually do have the ability to create. They make visible what is from the "Mind," what is *thought*, what is considered. And this is how change is enacted and this is how energy is moved and also created. It is in the power of the Mind, *thought*, the ability to conceive of, to create imagery, to even potentially create universes and dissolve universes with *thought*, that the "magician," the "wizard," the "Master" is defying the agreements of the Physical Universe. This (goes) back to the "conservation of energy."

Unfortunately, that's something that is still relayed in "metaphysics" and "magick" as it relates to the Physical Universe—it's still taught—this agreement with the "conservation of energy." Of course, I fell prey to that as well back in the 90's and those presentations—and I have no reason to change that because that is still the way Grade-I Route-A "Magick" is taught today: that you're still treating the concept that energy *is*, everything that *is* within the Physical Universe has already been, has already been given to (you), and you can't really do anything with it except move it around—you can't create it; you can't destroy it. It's been other-determinedly created for you and *that's that.*

And by contributing to this further agreement more and more: this is one of the trappings of "magick." So, of course, at a Master-level of understanding we know better than to do this. Because the truth is basically this: *thought*, the "Mind" and its connection between Spirit (the Self, Alpha-Spirit, I, I-AM...however you put that, who the individual actually is; their actual beingness) and this Body (which is just identified with)—it's really *thought* that is the communicative channel.

Other than the "control" and "power" and "discipline" of *thought*, there really is very little *to*, I'm sorry to say, a "magical paradigm"—fixing one's existence or conception of things *to* a "magical paradigm" or the study of "magick" for an entire lifelong pursuit [*laughs*] of just "magical traditions." If you can get the "thought discipline"—which I guess, we should probably get into a little bit more—but if you can get the "thought discipline" out of it when pursuing your Grade-I pursuit of "magick" then it won't be for all loss.

If... unfortunately your Seeker becomes very confined to having to work only within "magick circles" and only if they have access to their "four elemental weapons" or "tools" and only if the "stars are right," well, then you're going to be running into some issues if you're trying to move them along the *Pathway to Self-Honesty*. Because we know that such things are not the case as we get to higher and higher grades of development.

We know that these were just simply *considerations* to help fix some one's attention... It's just easier for disciplining the mind (this way), not that it is an absolute requirement. We go, "Oh, well... Friday is attributed to Venus and love and passion and emotion and... the color green" and so on and so forth. So you get an initiate to essentially focus and develop on these aspects during that time period. Say, well, "This is your time period to focus on this. This is class schedule for today: we're going to talk about emotion and we're going to talk about love and... the control of emotion, the ways in which emotional energy can be channeled or... transmitted or projected into various objects, and how easily it can be manipulated by even thought." ...things of that nature.

And it just gives a basic structure as one is developing, as one is moving away from confined limited considerations of just the Physical Universe. But now, if they come out of it with the thought that: okay, well I can only do a love spell on a Friday when Venus is visible in the sky and well, if I don't have this jasmine incense then it's going to fail..." and so on. And again, this is part of the trapping of the "magical system" that unfortunately, it's a step above believing that you can do nothing about it... I mean, it gets someone out of the idea that they're a victim, that they're constantly the effect of, that they have absolutely no control over their life or their destiny or the direction of energy.

But then again, it's a matter of stepping out of one box into another box of considerations and another set of paradigm semantics and restrictions—this is something that you want to make sure, as a Master, if you're going to be governing a Magic School or apprenticing Seekers and so forth, that you make sure they are not losing the value or the perspective that it's the Self that is *doing* these things; the Self that is able to connect with or communicate in any way.

This isn't something that... the significances, and all of the colors and the candles and the fragrances and the incense smoke and all the altar dressings are really applied only by the Mind. There is no other significances to them. It's material "material." It's physical universe material given consideration by the Self... It's dyed with whatever colors it is... Its only value is the ability to focus and concentrate the Mind on a given goal or a given target or concentrated focus on an object or manifestation, thought-form... whatever it is.

If it isn't actually contributing to that, then it is useless; it has no purpose in being in an individual's ritual or ceremony—I don't care what the "books" say; I don't care about what it says that the requirements are. The idea that... you know... these are all fragmentary memories of another existence.

There was another existence before this one. We all came from that one actually. And most people actually that are involved with the occult—that have any kind of relationship with the "New Age" and what not—really are just kind of *keying-in* or restimulating memories from this other existence, this other "Magical Universe" or "Magical Kingdom" as it's referred to sometimes in our Systemology at the highest levels.

And you don't necessarily need to get into this with your Seeker about this on a first grade level... I mean, this is, higher perspective work, but the point being that most people that have been involved with this, they've already had a strong relationship with the "Magical Kingdom" or "Magical Universe" and within that "Magic Kingdom" was able to employ... because the power of the electron, the consideration of energy and power, and power sources, in the "Magical Universe" were other than what we consider them here in the Physical Universe in beta-existence in *this* universe.

So, the idea of "wands," the idea of "intention," the idea of "thought" being able to direct... and all of the "regalia" that is attached to that, was actually something that actually served a greater intended purpose—and actually effective—*in* the "Magic Kingdom" of which in this existence we see only remnants and shadows of, and most people get attached to that.

In the "New Age" and the "occult" and "metaphysics, we're seeing the regalia, the cloaks, the staffs, the wands, all the magical tools, the concepts of the "tablets" and journeying and even, unfortunately using the [quote; unquote] "astral" as a substitution for what was once possible within the "Magic Kingdom." So, you have these "mythical creatures," "teleportation," all of this type of stuff... "astral traveling" or what not, that's considered esoteric or "occult" from a "New Age" perspective, because it isn't being manifested one-*to-one* within this material universe. I don't care *how* successful or adept, you know, "masterful" you are with these practices—don't let those other people fool you.

Of course this has become quite adamant in the rise of the internet and independent publishing. We see a lot of these quasi-cult leader central figures with their supposed claims and what not, you know, don't let them fool you... This "magical paradigm" stuff... unless you are breaking into the higher Systemological levels with it, all they are doing is coming up with further and greater ways of agreeing with the Physical Universe and the structure of the Physical Universe, so much as they want to impose it on the "Magical" one.

We'll get into that a little bit here soon when we talk about the elements, because in "elemental work" we see a bridge, again, between the type of stuff that's been carried through in terms of thought work and natural philosophy from Grade-I as it carries up through into higher levels—particularly as we cross over from Route-A to Route-D. One of the commonalities between "Magick and Mysticism" in Route-A, you're going to find when you look over *Great Magickal Arcanum*, particularly this edition, *The Master Course in Mag-*

gick for Modern Wizards and all of the materials and books that make up *Merlyn's Complete Book of Druidism* (Route-D), it's going to be the "elemental magick" stuff.

Another thing is anything that has to do with the Mind or *thought.* So, in our next lecture, we'll get into the structure of the universes as they relate to Mind of *thought* and use that as a bridge to get into the elemental work by the end of the day and hopefully get—really get—us into Route-D to stay on schedule here.

: LECTURE 10—MIND TECH :
(September 22, 2020)

So, in the last lecture I was actually discussing that I was working—in high school actually—on various concepts and, well it's actually the same time I was working with the "Elven Fellowship Circle of Magick." People are often confused because when I talk about my age, when I talk about the time period of which I've actually done a lot of this work, it seems conflicting, including my "Merlyn Stone" period and the time period in the 90's when I was self-publishing and doing a lot of work that way... seems unbelievable to some individuals, apparently.

But, yeah—so, anyways, in the 1990's, late 90's, it was 1999 when I was basically the guest speaker when I taught half-a-dozen "psychology" classes at my high school. And one of the first exercises I would open up the first class—the first presentation—by... there are a couple ways you could do this: you could have them record it as it was happening (which sometimes wasn't as effective for the reason of, that it would cause them to have to focus on writing during the time period, but then again, the recall...) or you could have them recalling it later (and that sometimes was not as effective because you had to depend on their ability to recall and their ability to remember).

So, I would take an egg-timer, which is usually about two minutes—so I would have them basically just "free think," just "free thought," "free associative thinking" and just... two-minutes of quiet and let them just have... let the mind scroll the various thoughts and things and whatever would take place.

And then afterward, I would have them record it: write down each individual thought—the chains—like "Oh, the math test I have tomorrow" or "I'm going to be going to work after school" and just whatever it was and list them. And then to assign whether positive or negative emotion is attached to the individual thoughts, with a "plus" or "minus" sign.

So, you know, you list this, and two-minutes of thinking and so... what it was meant to demonstrate—what it would usually demonstrate—was the amount of time... the amount of change in *thought*, unfocused *thought*, of just the free drifting of thought, you know, the various things that would just spontaneously (be) occupying thought. And then, of course, the emphasis on the negatives, because most people would have more "negatives" than "positives" in terms of thought.

That's one example of an exercise just to open up, you know, someone getting aware of, or some kind of relationship, with their thoughts. Because as I was mentioning previously, if you want to do your Seekers any good—especially from the Grade-I level of understanding and working towards higher levels and grades of Systemology—you want to give them "wins" by focusing on the techniques and exercises and basic training that emphasizes the "Mind," or emphasizes the discipline and concentration of *thought*. That's where you're going to get your biggest "wins" and your greatest benefit from the Grade-I material.

But what's actually introduced is really a basic exercise that goes back to when I was taking my own "Magick classes" and was in "Magic School" in the 90's. One of the first training exercises—in terms of thought control—would be to basically just *observe*—as an Observer, independent of—the train of thought that would be taking place for about five minutes.

These were weekly classes that I was attending, and so the idea was you'd practice for five minutes, and each day you would add an additional minute until you got to ten minutes. You would be basically observing just your train of thought and then replaying it—or at least making the strongest attempts to remember the thought stream that was taking place during the previous five or ten minutes.

The purpose was simply in being able to observe the Mind having this array of thoughts taking place, and of course, the more you did this, the more you realized that you as the I or Self *was* in fact an observer, which was looking at the various manifestations of the Mind and so forth.

So, at first it was really just a matter of observing—being able to observe the thought stream and being able to recall it and, of course, each day you would notice that the train of thought would become more concise; a little bit less chaotic; because you're putting more attention on the fact that you *are* observing the *thoughts*, so they're not running as random and actually tend to be less and less "mundane" as time goes on.

As more thought control is maintained, the aspects and facets contained in those thoughts tend to be a little higher level, higher levels of realization, less "thinking" more concerned with the gravity of the material universe. Really, the most important part is getting an individual to actually focus their attention on what the "body" is doing—get them in control of whatever the body is doing. And this starts with the "Mind"—getting them in control of what the Mind is doing at all times, whatever it's thinking about.

There are some exercises in advanced Systemology and our Systemology "processing" that has to do with the selective direction of attention. Of course, this is dealt with, like I said: it's one of the only real effective aspects of why "magickal development" actually works.

One of the things being, again, we talked about "thought control," so the actual focus of it and discipline of it being: to be able to maintain or hold a thought for extended periods of time. And this is critical whether you're dealing with "recall" and "advanced systemological processing" or even just the "occult" and "magickal" processing and tech that we're dealing with at Grade-I level, it really boils down the ability to hold thought.

And I was just talking to someone last night about this, where the separation between those that have advanced with metaphysics quite profoundly, or in magical paradigms, and those that really have had very little *reality* on it —it has to do with imagery, creative visualization, or just mental imagery in general. Some people actually have no real conception of mental imagery or thought control or anything of that nature, and so that's, again, one of the points in which "magick" and metaphysics and mysticism *can* be a bit of a step up at the *Lunar Level* (at the Grade-I level)   on the gateways... pathway... to actually elevate an individual in their ability to manage and control thought and creative imagery.

So, one of the next exercises would be to be able to basically "hold a thought." Now, we don't want to put any emphasis or any strength or solidity into reactive thinking, so whatever thought you would use for this exercise— whatever the first thought is that comes to mind, you just kind of want to throw that one away. It could be... I mean, eventually we want to work a person up to where they will able to actually manage and control their *thoughts*, overriding the reactive programming and so forth.

But at a "magical" level, you're basically just picking a thought. They used to use a lot of symbolism; a lot of objects; candle flames—things like that. It could really be just a matter of, you know, having like "this book is blue" or something of that nature.

So, you want to be able to take a *thought* and *hold* a thought —basically to discipline yourself to be able to maintain and concentrate on just a simple thought without any interference or reactivity or anything.

Of course, in the "psychology" class we were dealing with some basic exercises—but at a magical level, most will start with like five minutes and again you want to work yourself up to ten minutes in basically just being able to a hold a single concept or thought without any intrusion. And again, this for most individuals, this will take some practice. It's not one of the more "colorful" aspects of magical development, but it's one of the more effective ones; one of the ones that holds true as you work your way up the *Pathway*.

And then, of course, the next practice you would take up would be basically just the negation of *thought*; just absolute control of *thought* mechanisms or the Mind-Systems and negating *thought*. Now, in the previous exercise, you're giving an individual something to focus on, saying, "this book..." or "this candle..." or, you know, some object, and then saying "use this as a focus" and negate or, you know, focus on this in exclusion to all other *thoughts*.

The next step, of course, logically being to not even have that as the focus and just simply focus on the "non-activity"—to basically negate any intruding thoughts. This would basically fall under the [*laughs*]... in "mysticism" what you would consider "meditation" or simply the absolute control of thought; you don't need to put too much emphasis on this.

There's a lot of Eastern traditions that have spent an entire lifetime simply trying to "think" or "hold" an absence of thought or "think of Nothing" or so forth, and as far as I can tell, most of these individuals—even though they've been able to discipline the body to sit quite still or in the same position thirty years as they went into it with, have basically just gone out of this existence in that blanked-out state.

So I don't know that that's necessarily a form of development or something to emphasize, simply... anything that actualizes an actual emphasis on *thought* control—control of thought—and concentration. So, being able to control the flow of thoughts and the Mind-System, of course, and that leads *all the way* up into Systemology.

One of the elements that actually overlooked in a lot of—well except a few of the "Hermetic" paradigms and more advanced schools—is basically "Self-Analysis." This is something to integrate at a Grade-I level, as a magician is going into their basic developments of practice.

Our best method, actually, of this was only developed about a year ago at the Systemology Society. It appears in the "*Crystal Clear*" volume as the "Beta Awareness Test" and is also reprinted in the "*Systemology Handbook*" (the Master Edition), but it's really just to get a level of introspection and to consider the characteristics that an individual is carrying with them, which could be both positive and negative.

Now, interestingly enough, what we gear this towards—as we work towards the higher grades of Systemology—is really identifying elements, facets, programming or implants that pertain to a "personality." We know that there *is* an individual—an Alpha-Spirit, that is the I-AM or Self—but that many of the attributes, many of the facets, many of the aspects that an individual identifies with Self, are actually a part of an "artificial identity" or "personality."

This is one of the elements that really can actually "fast-track" a "magician" up the *Pathway of Self-Honesty*, because without really taking any time for introspection or looking at the aspects of "personality," most of the low-level or low-magical elements of the "magical tradition" will really only reinforce or solidify these other tendencies, which if they are artificial, again: I mean, an individual can do or not as they please, but unless they are actually free of some of these other attributes and personality programming, they are not actually acting as Self, they are acting within the perspective or point-of-view of the, you know, "colored glasses" of a particular "filter" or a particular "personality program."

This is, again, one of the trappings of the "magical systems"—the Grade-I work—is that if the individual isn't aware, or given the tools or the ability to be aware, the education, of these "personalities," these aspects, other filters of reality experience, they are only going to use the magical systems to further solidify this fragmentation of Self. And although it may seem to be at least above the mundane level of, for example, the Earth Gate—the Physical Universe or beta-existence—it's going to solidify them into just the personality programming that they already are carrying with them, just at a little bit more of a higher superpowered level.

Now there are a few other elements of basic "magical development," magical training and tech that I presented in "*The Power of Zu*" lecture series nearly a year ago. The transcripts for *The Power of Zu*, they were released by themselves, but also they appear in the "*Systemology Handbook*" and also your "Instructor's Manual" as the bridge to Grade-III.

And there is a lot of information in that concerning the "power of breath" and, you know, the "basic magical regimen" and "care of the body" in terms of "energetic reception" in terms of the "health and cleanliness," the "diet" and so forth. And a lot of that is treated as the ability to maintain, basically, a healthy "genetic vehicle" just for the fact... not that bodies are so important, but for the fact that it's been found to be the case time and time again that an individual is going to be fixed in their attentions on the physical body when it's ailing them—or when it's having issues or...

For example, cleanliness isn't maintained, then the proper reception of oxygen, the proper reception of breathing through the pores—in terms of control of breath—these elements are all taken up in *The Power of Zu* lectures and they're very critical for both the "magical development," higher grade "Hermetic mysteries," and then also, again, they were presented to the Systemological Society nearly a year ago and are considered part of the bridge from these other "routes" to Grade-III "Mardukite Systemology."

"Autosuggestion" or "Auto-conditioning" is frequently taught in schools of "Hermetic Mysteries," however as of the developments—the 2019 and of course 2020 developments—of "Systemology," auto-conditioning is no longer a recommended practice. I mean, it can be explored for the nature of what it is. Unfortunately, it really only reinforces programmed reactive-response tendencies of the Human Condition.

You're changing and altering them—but it's really a form of "self-hypnosis." Now, this was originally something we were using as, like, a marketing tool—or a thema—for classifying, for example, the *Crystal Clear* book. But "self-hypnosis" and "autosuggestion" is really not a preferred practice as of a "Master-level" understanding of our research and discovery.

In most cases, it's recommended that a Seeker keep some kind of "magical diary" or—it doesn't have to be a "grimoire" per say, although it's clear that these magical notebooks, diaries, records of experiments and experiences are what later contributed to popular grimoires and probably the classification of "magical correspondences."

In Systemology we actually have the *Truth Seeker's Adventure Journal*, which is actually a "processing notebook" or a "processing record" that keeps track of the experiences that a Seeker has when they're doing "systematic processing." And you keep track of, naturally, date and time—and also astrological significances if they are significant to an individual—the practices and then different realizations, circumstances, events that are taking place... and also any experiments, mental imagery, creative visualization exercises... anything that can be kept track of, to basically treat the pursuit of magic, mysticism and all the way through the higher grades as an academic or intellectual pursuit.

I mean, this isn't something that you need to spend a lot of time rigorously working out as a—as you would for example, in an academic setting for historical purposes and dates, times and a lot of arbitrary data—but we do treat, at the Master-level of understanding with the inclusion of historical understanding in Grade-II with Mardukite Mesopotamia, and then of course the future of spiritual evolution and development of the Human Condition that we have in Systemology.

There's really no limit to what we can fixedly structure our understanding for, when it comes to the Physical Universe, so these "magical notebooks," "magical diaries"—however, you want to refer to them—these "personal notebooks," *grimoires*, they simply assist one in treating this as a reality, something to increase their understanding, their communication, their reality, on these subjects, and to be able to articulate them, again, communicate them, to other individuals.

So, that's very important—because a lot of times this work becomes a little bit exclusive—an individual runs the risk of becoming overly introspective, and basically kind of collapsing into themselves if they really have no frame of reference with the commonality or some kind of base or plane of communication with other individuals. Otherwise it becomes very self-oriented and, you know, a person can become almost *overly* individuated where they end up basically withdrawing from the game of the Physical Universe.

And we see this more and more in the practices or the instruction in the Eastern thought, but it's just as commonly found in the West, when an individual basically loses touch with the environment around them; the inability to separate the personal universe and the Mind-System from the external physical beta-existence that is taking place around us.

One of the shortcoming of the term "visualization" or

"mental imagery" is that it pertains only to the "visual" aspects of what's called into Mind, when of course we know from our work from Systemology that there's actually quite a few facets that are combined with that.

So, anything—exercises, thought discipline—anything—concentration—that pertains to actually getting a sense of, or an artificial sense of, creating various scenes, sounds, the sensations that you might feel, as far as touch, anything you might smell, taste... basically improving an individual's (basic) ability to create these or have control of them in the Mind—and of course we have associations with the same, when we come to "systemological processing."

We know that each of these *facets* has associated knowledge and other programming associated to it that's reactive-response based. So, any of those exercises that pertains to that—so, getting in at the ground floor in Grade-I, establishing that the concept of visualization and mental imagery—in spite of the name or the semantics of that—is to pertain to the other *facets* or, well, we refer to them as *facets* in Systemology, but the other "senses" and "perceptions" that are associated with the same. Not just specifically "visual" only, so...

Anything that can be employed that involves strengthening of Willpower is, of course, significant. This just involves, again, maintaining control over the actions of the body—anything that's automatic, anything that's reactive-response oriented. Being able to basically enact a greater control over the "identity" that unfortunately Self has become too closely attached to.

We deal with trying to separate more and more of this as time goes on in the grades, but some basic elements of this, even for example, the compulsions, are just automaticities of, for example, feeling hungry. If an individual is used to just feeling or something triggers an urge or something and they're used to "oh, well, getting up and walking to grab some food" or something—to be able to actually maintain some control of *willingness* and *knowingness* in terms of the actions of the body; to be actually... to control that.

We're not talking about depriving...you know, starving yourself or something; but basically just maintaining some basic control over the automatic functions of the body—these are all... fall within the domain of "magical development" at a high level—you know, when you start treating the "Hermetic" or the "thought exercise" level of the Mind.

Another thing you're gonna run into—in terms of training or point of development—here, I've seen it referred to as the "Witches' Triangle" or "Wizard's Pyramid." It's actually based on an old Welsh Triad of the Bardic Druids—but the basic aspects or pillars: to *know*, to *dare* and *be silent* and so on. There's actually even an old—from the old concepts of Solomon's temple—that it was built on four pillars: *knowledge, courage, volition* and *silence* and that it was somehow the microcosm and macrocosm of all the temples, or of which the "Hermetic" sciences were built.

But, really—so, when we deal with *knowingness*, there's several aspects of *knowingness* and they actually boil down really to an individual's ability to "*be*" in order to "*know.*" *Being* something—"Being" of course, the highest echelon of knowledge—to "*Know*" what something is.

The other aspect of this: there's, you know, we have to persevere and be tenacious in terms of the pursuit of knowledge. One of the other traps of the "magical paradigm" is to essentially *crave* knowledge insatiably. Because there's always one more "magickal correspondence" or one more "spell" or one more piece of "information" that's always *needed* to complete the picture. Because, of course, as a paradigm, it's still fairly engrossed in "mystery"—in the *Unknown*. And so it can always be fragmented, as has been relayed in countless books that I've written—that it's just insatiably fragmented further and further.

And then of course, that's *to know*, and then *to dare*—we're to... basically imply or enforce one's Will on the experience that one has—Willpower on the experience one has as an individual—and to be able to basically push through to establish a sense of Self; Self that is steadfast and not restricted to any one or another paradigm, or to the opinions of others in terms of what's considered real or unreal or possible or impossible.

These are all *agreements* with the Physical Universe that a "magician" is obviously pitted up against in their practice. And then, of course, this all comes together when we refer to the final part of it—to *be silent*—because really, and we deal with this again more specifically at higher grades of Systemology, but when it comes to the command and control of the Mind-System—the Mind-Body connection; the experience of reality in the Physical Universe—what we find most detrimental, when it comes to programming and an individual's desire to reach and withdraw, to create and move along the *Pathway to Self-Honesty*, has to do with "invalidation" and the "invalidation" that's been taken on from others.

Now, when an individual is strong enough, they can usually take on or withstand more and more of this without succumbing to the pressures and feeling it as an attack on the integrity of who they are as an individual. But, in the development of Grade-I work or an individual's first steps on the *Path* or even initially when they are working on Systemology and the processing, it's really better just to be *silent* when it comes to other people, because we really want an individual to be as strong as they can and stand on their own before trying to take that on; take on the potential invalidation of others.

We're not trying to impose or suggest some kind of "disconnect" or, you know, the seclusion or removing people from their environment or their family or anything of that nature.

However, when they are trying to develop and they are trying to work on these things and they are trying to get along with this, originally, it does seem that it's just better for them to work on it quietly and not to boast about anything or really try to bring other people into that—that essence of their reality—until their reality is strong enough to take on the Awareness and opinions and attentions of other individuals.

[*Okay, let's take a break.*]

: LECTURE 11—MAGICAL ELEMENTS :
(September 22, 2020)

So we've come to a crossroads in the curriculum then—in the *Pathway*—because it's been laid down here, which is essentially "elementalism." When we talk about a bridge or some kind of connectivity between Route-A and Route-D on Grade-I, you're talking about the "elements."

It is true the "elements" play a role in "ritual magic," all of the fundamentals of "magick." They incorporate it into the "spellcraft" traditions—*Wicca* and *Witchcraft*. They're involved in the ceremonial magic of the Golden Dawn and experimentation with *grimoires* and things of that nature.

My personal—when I've treated apprenticeships, magical curriculums in the past—my personal way of going about this has actually been to treat the "magical" part or "Magic School" as generically as possible. And by that I mean, the rudiments, the fundamentals, such as the Mind-Tech that we were talking about, principles of just specific-generic development; not anything that's specific to any paradigm or specific tradition of that in that sense.

So, when I've involved "elemental magic" or the "elements" or *Elementalism* as I became fond of calling it—that was really an inherent part of the "Druid School," which was an extension of the "Magic School." Before I even had all these grades set up for, like, the Master Course or the Academy and some of the work in Systemology—in the past, I was actually dividing an entry-level "Magic School" apprenticeship that was meant to open up to what became a "Druid School."

And this was actually plotted back in the 90's when some of the original "ritual magic" circles and groups and *covens* that I was involved with—I ended up moving it towards what became the *Elven Fellowship Circle of Magick* for several years and the materials that were explored in not only the *Sorcerer's Handbook*, but the transition that was taking place toward the *Druid's Handbook*, and then eventually what became the material in the *Elvenomicon*.

The *Druid's Handbook*, the *Elvenomicon* materials, the *Draconomicon*, my *Pheryllt* research, and another work—the *Pantheisticon*—all appears in the Master Edition of *Merlyn's Complete Book of Druidism: A Master Course in Druidry for Modern Druids*.

Now there is a basic synthesis of rudiments within the *Sorcerer's Handbook* that was a part of the original "Magic School" curriculum—primarily to introduce, just the concept of the "elements" and this is actually expanded in the *Great Magickal Arcanum* material.

But really, in the *Sorcerer's Handbook*, other than introducing the "elements," symbols and "Signs of Portal" for the *elements* we use in ritual magic, and then since the chapter also crosses with Druid tradition, we also introduce "basic tree energy" work and "basic tree communication" and just, the format of incorporating the elements and "elementals" into ritual—and that's about the extent to where I would take "elemental magic" as part of the "Magic School."

And then again, Route-D being specifically tied to Druid tradition and the Elven tradition—the Celtic Faerie Tradition—things of that nature, which can be a separate series of classes; separate series of courses. Just as I've separated them, so to speak, in delivering *this*.

The most fundamental—if you want to talk about what is the fundamentals of the criteria for introducing *Elementalism*—you've got Earth, Air, Fire and Water. And then we also refer sometimes to this quintessential quintessence—fifth element—perfected unification of it all and so on and so forth, also as "Akasha."

Just to give you a brief rundown as it appears in the *Sorcerer's Handbook* on this list: you got Earth providing structure, substance and foundation. Basically solidity. And then in the midst of that, as it applies to Life and so on, it's the "keys" to abundance and growth.

The element of Air: specific to communication, illumination, focus, clarity. Basically the mental faculties, intellect, knowledge and so on; tied to the Air. With Fire, I mean this almost goes without saying—I mean some of this is pretty intuitive—so, strength, courage, vitality; basically as an active force, protection; the kind of fiery passions also.

And then Water, of course, being transformation, healing, purity and then here it says, the "keys" to inner peace. We consider that, when we look at water, also the tranquility—and then also kind of a "gate" back to other aspects of ourselves or hidden aspects of ourselves: emotions that aren't necessarily as fiery.

So, you got Fire and Water being very fluid and vibrant in that respect and then Earth and Air on the other end of that. Now, these are explored in so many different ways and in so many different contexts.

I mean, I've established—when I was doing my first "standard model," and this predates the Standard Model of Systemology—when I had established that, I was actually more involved or more interested I should say, in trying to unify "metaphysics" with "quantum physics."

I've no longer really pursued the physical sciences as a means—once we kind of cracked the code of Systemology work, which took almost a decade going on behind the scenes while all this other Mardukite and developments were taking place.

I was more concerned with the way that it could be relayed or the way it could be unified or brought to or communicated to those that were more involved with the physical sciences that were still mainly dealing with agreements with the Physical Universe.

And so I thought that "quantum physics" and "string theory" and "dimensional theory" and so forth was going to be a bridge to that; a bridge to maybe a better understanding of what these higher realizations could be accessed. And so, you'll see a lot of that in *The Great Magickal Arcanum* actually; you'll see sections that are dealing with *grimoires* and these visualization exercises and various incantations, back-to-back with articles that I wrote trying to stuff in specifically to "grand unified theories" and "quantum physics" and "metaphysics" and "epistemology" and various philosophical schools.

The *Great Magickal Arcanum* is really—it's actually [*laughs*] a little bit ahead of its time, given that it was considered a Grade-I foundation, because most of the higher elements can be found in there. I mean, that work was developed between 2006 and 2008, and by 2008, I was already working on launching the founding of the Mardukite Ministries at its inception. And so I was already looking towards the next grade, and I had that all in the back of my head while I was really working on *Arcanum*.

So, you see a lot of integration of the Druidry, Mesopotamia, and what eventually ended up becoming Systemology—though it isn't really classified as such in that book. You do see a lot of those elements already very much evident; very much being presented in the *Arcanum* material.

Now, my model at the time—and this was integrated back into the *Sorcerer's Handbook*; it wasn't in the original edition, but it's in the 21st anniversary edition; it's also in the new edition of *Great Magickal Arcanum* (the Master Edition here; big hardcover)—and so what I did was connect the element of Earth with the force of gravity. And the element of Air with electromagnetism.

And see, gravity is really a property of mass—or mass being a property of gravity, depending on how you look at that—and that I tied to Earth, particularly regarding "matter" as basically a passive force. Just as it's observed in the "elemental tradition." And then with Air, we're talking about electromagnetism, we're talking about vibrations—we're talking about the entire electromagnetic spectrum there, which is actually traveling, its moving points, particles, moving as a wave function through the air.

The weak nuclear force I attached to Fire. And, of course, the weak nuclear force being like "radiation"—what you would really consider like the fiery force there of explosions and the radioactivity that comes from that, the decay of nuclear particles. And then for Water we have strong nuclear, which is the other nuclear force, and that's the one that is actually what bonds the masses and vibrations and radiations together to create this kind of "sea" or "fabric" of space so to speak. They all kind of interrelate.

So, back in like 2008—I had developed it earlier than that, but I released it in *The Great Magickal Arcanum*—as a basic "elemental model" that could be employed not only functionally for mystical purposes, but also to show a correspondence—and I actually kind of, my own miniature model of a "Grand Unified Theory"—concerning the elements and their manifestations as we are most rigidly experiencing them in the Physical Universe.

Now in the more "Celestial" traditions—the Grade-II type work—where you see "rising on higher planes" and things that are working above the Earth Gate, most of the cosmology and models that you'll find is more specifically geared towards the planets. So, you'll see more of the sevenfold—or some kind of kabbalistic model to that effect—but the purposes of Grade-I, whether it's ritualistic systems, explorations into magick or even "Route-D" into Druidism—the work of Druidry—the natural magics, the natural philosophies, that which was kind of geared towards understanding our place in the Physical Universe or Self in the Physical Universe, the structure of the Physical Universe and its overlay into higher metaphysical ideals, is real tied down into the elemental systems.

You'll see this in a lot of models anyways. You'll see this on the Kabbalah. You'll see this in high and ceremonial magic. You'll see this in a lot of methods of relaying even higher cosmologies and various planes and—if you want to call them "dimensions." But down here at the bottom of this base here, you'd see this "square" and it's divided actually—it's got this "X" in it—it's divided into four triangles, and they're each colored in a different color, which are basically a representation of the structure of the Physical Universe.

Now, it's often superimposed as being the structure of the "Magical Universe," but we kind of assume that there is some kind of relationship or relay in that—that these forces and basic streams and currents have somehow just become more solidified and condensed.

Of course, when we're treating the energetic aspects—whether it's in ritual or visualizations, dealing with the "elemental forces," energies, entities and so on—we're not necessarily treating the physical manifestations of these elements as they would be most solidly understood.

For example, the element of Fire is present in an understanding of things that beyond just the actual physical representation of, like, a "flame" and so forth. The models are used as a way of codifying and understanding and very loosely systematizing—I mean, the Druids were the systematizers of the Celtic people and essentially Western knowledge. Earlier we had systematizers from the Ancient Near East that their traditions and secret knowledge became popularized in the Egypto-Grecian, like the Greek "Hermetic" tradition—and classical mythology too [*laughs*]—but classical "philosophers."

Given those like Pythagoras and Aristotle and so forth—these are given credit for widely distributing and publishing writings, or having their dialogues recorded and written, such as with Plato and Socrates; they become, in our traditional understanding of history and the textbooks, the origins behind all this. It seems like suddenly this "classical world" was the one that developed and came up with all of this knowledge when it actually came from thousands of years prior.

We can look at ancient records *now* and understand that, however, as you can tell, the history books and what's being taught in school or what's mainstream is very slow to catch up.

There's several ways and sequences in which *Elementalism* can be relayed to a Seeker. If you're going to be working with—now that we're working or moving into Grade-I Route-D—the structure that's presented in the *Druid's Handbook*, which is also within *Merlyn's Complete Book of Druidism* there, is: Earth, Water, Air, Fire.

And what this does is actually move an individual out from the most physical to the most spiritual or to the most fluid. So, you got Earth being the most solid; that which you're grounded in—and then Water being another tangible; almost a liquid version of solids. And then Air, which is the—can also be connected to "space" and the four directions and all that kind of stuff. And then Fire being in many elements, a combination.

In some systems of *Elementalism*, the Akasha—the "Divine Spark" or Fire or the quintessence of it all—was actually an extension *of* the Fire element. Because, of course, the Fire element, you have oxygen, you have moisture, you have the smoke and vapors, the combusted material—all of that pre-

present in order to make Fire. You know, when we study this stuff as kids: the "triangle" of the Fire, and you take out the Air and you don't have it, or you take out the material and you don't have it and so on and so forth.

Well, that kind of concept was actually derived from "natural philosophy." Natural philosophy being an early predecessor to the physical sciences. It was basically the mystics and wizards and magicians and priests and priestesses and shamans and so forth—those that were basically more intellectual; less mundane oriented in societies—and they would go out and they would simply observe; observe Nature. And they would kind of make their assumptions or classifications and correspondences based on these observations—and also cycles and various things.

This led *to* the concrete physical sciences that we have today.

Now if you're going to be treating these subjects at an academic level—meaning at an Academy level, if you're going to be teaching these courses—we've talked about "Magic School" and also, like, a "Druid School," you're gonna want personal involvement on the Seeker's part, in terms of understanding and putting these connections together. This is very important. It's one of the only reasons why some of these mystical elements actually work within a "magical paradigm": there is a personal understanding that is involved with these models.

Rather than just becoming completely engulfed in what symbols and the symbolism and the tools and some of these objective aspects, the best thing you can do when it comes to the *Elementalism*, is to basically have a Seeker creating models for themselves of this paradigm as a continuity.

So, drawing a circle—drawing a circle, putting a cross through it—and traditionally we've divided them... in a ritual sense, we've divided them into four quarters. So you got

North, South, East and West. So, in North, you have Earth; and in the East you have Air; and in the South, you have Fire; and in the West you have Water.

Now, you can either, you know, get a nice piece of poster-paper or poster-board or large surface and draw a big one out and just sit and copy in every single, you know, possible correspondence you can find in there—or you can take these apart, bit by bit, you know, looking at them as cycles. Because again, that's the whole point of the demonstration of the (continuity) Circle.

Not only is it a representation of the manifest universe as we are participating in it as a game field, but when you look at the "threshold periods" and "threshold keys" as they're given in the textbooks here, you've got, for example, not just North, South, East and West as a continuity of space, you've got also the chronology of *time*, which is very significant to the ancient pagan human being—for the one purpose that their survival depended on agriculture, so their ability to chart time and work alongside the time was something that kind of keyed them in to being ingrained into the Earth—into the Earth Systems; being Earth-aligned.

With "threshold times," you've—I've actually charted a few, but I'm sure there's many other ways you can divide and fragment *Elementalism*—but, for example, up at the top we have North here, and we could put "midnight." Midnight turns into "dawn" or "sunrise" or morning-time over here in the East, which is also where the Sun rises; in the East.

And then you go down here to South and that would be Fire, which is also noon-time, which would be your hottest driest point of the day. And then over here in the West, you would have "dusk" going into twilight, represented by Water, and of course the Sun actually does set in the West. And then of course we go back into evening. You can do the same thing here with the seasons. Up here, with midnight and North and Earth and, you know, the dark and the cold, you can have "winter." And then you move down over here and you have the East and Air and the morning-time and these new beginnings and you have "spring." And then you move down here to the South and you've got Fire and noon-time and the heat and the dryness, well, there you have "summer." And as things cool off and begin to transition into another change cycle over here in the West, you have the "autumn" and, of course, the darkening, the sunset, the twilight and all that.

These models—this is not an arbitrary system obviously. *Elementalism* was a very concise way of observing the cycles and the patterns and that which was taking place *in* the natural world around. And this eliminated—rather than, you know, it was taught in the Ancient Mystery School traditions—but this eliminated the "Mystery."

This eliminated the *Unknowns.* And this allowed for higher and higher ideals to be reached for, not having to muddle around looking at, you know, the splicing atoms and trying to separate the Earth element into how many different particles and elemental qualities it could possibly have on a periodic table and so on and so forth.

Because what of—well, you know, if we look at this from the wizard's perspective and the metaphysical perspective—what has all this gained? What has all this material knowledge and the physic... the agreements with the Physical Universe and fractionating this Mystery into more and more... what is actually done for the Human Condition?

The Human Condition has actually become more and more entrapped, of course, and then keyed-into this Earth existence—this physical existence—and then to treat it as only the physical considerations of existence; excluding all concepts of the Mind, all concepts of the Spirit, concepts of a spiritual existence or an alternate universe.

So, what the ancient philosopher did, was have about as basic and perfected understanding *of* what was taking place in the universe and the physical existence around them, to put it *at rest*, to put it to *bed*, so they could actually pursue higher matters. And that's why a lot of their teachings and so forth became—I mean, these became what was originally this, you know, esoteric, very priestly, and occult, Hermetic, philosophical concepts... became the rudiments of the physical sciences down the road, it was just that they were really only understood of people back then and they would gather together in caves and these secret places.

They knew that they could really only speak to one another about these concepts, so rather than having to sit there and battle the masses and the opinions of the masses over and over and over again in which to make any headway, these higher minds would simply gather together amongst themselves; they had their own paradigms, their own semantics, their own languages, their own... passwords and secret handshakes—all of which basically to preserve a forum for them to develop what ended up later becoming the philosophies and sciences that, you know, we now have so easily taken for granted.

But I guarantee you: it is not the common man, it is not the guy that's putting one foot in front of the other and never questioning beyond what is placed right in front of them, that has made all of these advancements and understandings and new realizations in the last *6000* years. Again, these have always come out from the underground; they've come out from secret corners and recesses of society, but they're not the things that people are going to school to learn how to change or how to improve in any way, shape or form.

That was—I discuss that, back almost a year ago, in the *Power of Zu* lectures. And those transcripts are actually in your "Instructor's Manual." The education system—and, you know... I wasn't educated to be educated. I was one of those that barely made it through high school, and here I do... talking to you, doing these classes for the last twenty years, writing these books and so forth...

This is not the stuff you go to school for—but that is the whole point of what we are doing now. We're delivering the Mardukite Master Course for the Mardukite Academy of Systemology, *now* for the first time in modern history, there is a way to go to school for this—and to actually learn how to think for yourself for a change instead of having to think how others have thought for however many years and which has only brought us to lower and lower points of consideration.

Now the "magickal correspondences" are something that can get you into a little bit of sticky trouble depending on what background your Seeker actually has before coming to the "Magic Schools" or "Druid Schools," because—you know, back in the 90's, this is one of the reasons why [*laughs*] I systematized a standard universal methodology of "magick," which was originally presented as the *Sorcerer's Handbook* and expanded for the *Arcanum*, but I had... back in the 90's, I had been exploring so many different paths, traditions—been involved with so many different groups—and in that time saw just about each element and each correspondence of magick *corresponded* to or *correlated* to just about every other correspondence or element or color.

You know, I saw models where Earth was represented by this color and that color; and this one would be represented as the total opposite in the next model... and each one, was really able to, I guess in some respects, "qualify" itself for its paradigm. I mean, it would be able to make sense for those traditions, but as far as presenting a "universal standard," it became clear to me that... there really *wasn't* one [*laughs*].

And so that's something—when you see the work in *Arcanum*—and well really all the Grade-I work was really to establish a standard of the types of work that people were already involved in, whether it be the conventional contemporary "magick" and mysticism, or the "Druidic" and nature traditions—it was to present a standard.

So, for my purposes, I've always—if we're dealing with the most fundamental colors—I mean, there's alternative colors too that can be incorporated with that, or others in the spectrum (other shades and gradients), but I've always treated the Earth as the "green world" with the color green; and then Water, of course, blue; and Fire, red; and then I've used yellow for Air. And for twenty-five years that's been the basic methodology that I've applied to the elements in terms of color.

The same with "elemental beings"—you'll see with the mythological and classical beings: the *jinns* and *gnomes* and all that kind of stuff. There's various correspondences—you'll see them listed in the *Druid's Handbook* (which is in your Route-D textbook there) and *Arcanum* and all of—pretty much all these... they all have the "standard universalist magical tradition" applied to them, that I was working in the 1990's on, then kind of culminated in... after the new millennium with the *Druid's Handbook*, which was released underground in 2000 actually and 2001.

Surprisingly most of these materials were not taken up by mainstream publishers before I started up my own Press again. Because I was doing it in the 90's as "Merlyn Stone" which was also published. My family was even involved in helping assisting making that possible. I started pursuing third-party publishing, but really I think that now that we've established the Mardukite Academy, we've established the Joshua Free Imprint as a publishing company, we've established this Systemology Society—we've been able to be fairly self-managed in our endeavors and I can see this only continuing further on into the future in that direction.

: LECTURE 12—ELEMENTAL TECH :
(September 22, 2020)

[*Well, I promised we'd get into Grade-I Route-D by the end of today. This is our last lecture (for the day). The best way that I can do that—and keep with following the schedule that we had planned—is really just to continue on with our discussion on "Elemental Tech." Because this is applicable to both "routes" on Grade-I. And then we can actually take up—we'll start off first thing tomorrow with the "Route of Druidism."*]

Although there's a lot of different "Hermetic" sources behind it, the traditional classical philosophies are really what ended up dividing the "fourfold elemental systems" as we understand it. So, you've got: Earth, Air, Fire and Water; and of course, there's many ramifications to what this represents. Of course, I was referring to a few of them in the last lectures and the representations of the cycles of *time*.

But, of course, Earth being *more* than being just the "planet" Earth, or being a representation of the same concept—the solidity, perhaps. Again, Fire (as an element) meaning *more* than just the physical "flame"; Air being *more* than just the "oxygen" and, of course, Water being more than just "lakes" and "ponds" and such.

These elements have—although they have points of manifestation at beta-existence and a concrete physical level—that the essence that we can put, to have a continuity, that these represent in some aspect or in some combination, that we can classify all the phenomenon and all of the existence that we can experience with some way of bringing it back to these correspondences. This is something that became the subject of the "mystical" schools—the basis of them—and including the early physical sciences, all the way even back into the origins of "alchemy" and "chemistry" (that you can read about in the *Arcanum* book).

Prior to the inception of, for example, our modern idea of "physics" and the classification of physics, the basic conditions on which the elements were placed by the ancients, were basically boiled down to things such as "hot" and "cold" and "moist" and "dry" and you see these elements, actually, in early forms of herbal alchemies and so forth.

So, you have the element of Air, which is hot and moist; you have the element of Fire, which is hot and dry; you have the element of Earth, which is dry and cold; and then you have the element of Water, which is cold and moist. And so that was a classification that they had for that.

The only issue really with that, is that the model on which it's presented, doesn't always match up—it doesn't match up well with the standard directional and seasonal cyclic models. You would almost have to draw some jagged lines going through it to connect the elements on such a circular model.

Obviously the alchemical aspects—the physical manifestations of the elements—the models that were used, are different than the ones that are applied for metaphysical purposes, in terms of these models: the one, is where you're experiencing observations; and one, which you're enacting change. And, of course, the "alchemist" is always concerned with change and transformation.

When they are represented as concentric spheres—if you consider the Cosmic Elements as having a certain kind of fluidity or manifestation or connectivity with the "personal identity continuum" or the "Standard Model" (the Zu-line) as we approach it in Systemology—it's one of the reasons why I profess to basically use the Earth, Water, Air, Fire, and then Akasha *ordering*.

Because if you were to put them in these all—if you see here this diagram I made—the Earth being the "physical," basically centered focused continuity of the "Physical Universe," the beta-existent Physical Universe manifest. Water being just above that, applies to, for example, the RCC—the "Reactive Control Center"—the emotional (or misemotional) portions of the "personal identity continuum," which is the lower reactive-response mechanisms that are basically tied to the moving tides over this Earth-point—this center point —of physical continuity.

Then we move up between... Air, of course, being an aspect of the intellect, the Mind and so, the MCC—the "Master Control Center"—the "Mind" center, the analytical center of the Mind-System as we demonstrate it in the "Standard Model" would apply there. So, then Fire being the spiritual element, in essence, the fluid one of Self and Spirit; the one that occupies outside or exterior this interior beta-existence.

The Alpha existence is Fire, of which the All-encompassing would be the ALL; All of which is ALL. [*Laughs*] There's just an ALL, which is the "Fifth Element" or the quintessence.. of which is only... outside of which is being? [*mmhmm, yeah...*] The Infinity of Nothingness in our Cosmic Model—our "Standard Model of Systemology." So, you see you *can* apply the "elemental" methodology *to* this "Standard Model of Systemology" as well.

So you wanna give Seekers some reality on the elements then... and... I would say, again, let's start with the Earth —"Earth-in-Mind-Training" from the *Druid's Handbook* and *Merlyn's Complete Book of Druidism.*

So, you've got the most physical of the elements—and it's not just a representation of planet Earth, again. It's the physical bodies, living components, the idea of a wholeness —a continuity of wholeness—again, the manifestation of beta-existence. So, we might as well—some of the things attached to that, this way you can feel like we... this *is* a Master Course in "magick" in respects... and feel like we've talked about some of these things, right?

Trees, stones, animal work, shamanism, herbalism... the correspondences of gems, totems—anything significant to "Earth-oriented" traditions—this all falls under the domain of the Earth element. Also, domestics. The Earth is our home, also our dwelling places—anything that has to do with the family-unit: fertility, stability, abundance, growth... all of that pertaining to Earth.

We consider Earth to be, in many respects, the "Mother." There's also an "Earth Goddess," the "Gaia-system," the "Primeval Dragon," "Tiamat" we explore in Grade-II being "cut in twain." We'll talk a bit about that in relation to the *Draconomicon* and the "Dragon Tradition" for the Grade-I, so we'll be talking about that soon.

Then, also the Earth represents the "homes" or "buildings" or "bodies" of the actual traditions. Whether it's a "henge of stones" or "grove of trees," this type... the "Temple." This is always usually—I mean, "clay." Clay in Mesopotamia and the bricks in Egypt. You're seeing the "solidity," the manifestation of the element of Earth being used for that, to construct that.

Also, in the expression of the "Green World," we're talking about the land, soil, plant-life—the living creatures that feed and depend on that—that's all part of the "Green World" system. And so, when you're talking about "magick" and "Druidism" and when you're talking about the nature of traditions, really it's the Earth-oriented focus that seems to have most of that iconic imagery attached to it.

And then, of course, as a solid object or ritual tool, you have usually "stones" or a "pentacle" of some sort—and some of you, of course, know that the "pentacle" represents the elements in general; the physical elements and "man's solidity" as an embodied by these elements—and the experience of physical existence.

Now, if you're incorporating the higher levels of Systemology or A.T. work—the Actualized Technician work—of the "Wizard" levels of Systemology, you're of course gonna be involving "imagination" and projection of the "point of view." So, if you want to incorporate that at higher levels—or into your training—you're trying to project point-of-view, in the essence of the Earth, to get them to actually conceive of this solidity of the Physical Universe; doesn't have to consider that this is *all* that there is, or anything of that nature in terms of the reality of it—the ability to actually conceive of a condensed... the heavy condensed gravity of the Earth Element: substance—that which has the pull which brings us, basically, to [*laughs*] the considerations that we're entrapped in these "physical bodies."

We of course—I mean most of us here have been "processing" out of that—but those listening, or those that you're going to be teaching or instructing or processing as Seekers, they're still working through some of this. So you can have them imagine that the totality of Earth would extend to the farthest extents of the universe; that it was all—not just like planets spread out or a bunch of earth or clay—but that the dense Earth gravity, the heaviness, the substance, the thickness of it, is actually the full extent of existence; that it just goes as far into all directions. That would be the Earth Elemental Plane.

Unfortunately—and the kind of irony behind this—is that the Earth Elemental Plane, in that respect as it's been described, is actually the *next lowest* consideration for a beta-existence for the Human Condition. So—you know, that's one of those things: if we don't get this one right *here* as things have condensed and solidified and been considered to this point, the next—basically the next "prison universe" or "penalty universe" down is essentially, what some have referred to as the "mud universe," but it's basically: as much as you can consider the dark space of *this* existence going in all directions, it's just that thick syrupy condensed, basically "rock"... existence.

And so, this is something that can be visualized and imagined. I mean, we consider the epitome, actually, of Grade-IV, which goes beyond the "Master Course," but we consider that the ability to imagine—free consideration of imagination without inhibition, reactivity—is actually one of the pinnacle points that's going to get an individual *out* of the entrapment of solely rigid fixed point-of-view of the Human Condition.

This is something that you can actually begin to work with—within the Master levels; within the "Magic Course" or "Druid School" and begin to apply higher level realizations to these materials, which was not always put forth directly as they were set down—whether it was back in the 1990's or, you know, whatever ten or fifteen years ago, when I wrote these materials.

The point wasn't to keep ratifying and revising and so on and so forth; they are completely valid for the paradigms in which they've been presented as—whether it be Druidry or "ritual magick" or what have you, but that doesn't mean that in this time and in this work that we've done in, for example, the Systemology Society, that we haven't come to some greater heights, higher ledges of knowing and new realizations concerning all this stuff that came before.

That's one of the purposes of the "Master Course" here, because we're actually able to accelerate an individual—where they don't necessarily need to spend decades or a lifetime kind of pilfering through all this, this mess, to get to these realizations. But still get to them on their own.

We're not just feeding—hand feeding—the realizations to them; they... it's just that when the material and the attention is selectively directed and employed and effectively used, well then it's going to—it's actually going to come to them, as opposed to those which actually don't know what's going on and don't really have these realizations, but they've become popular with whatever marketing or books or materials or schools or that they've got. And with all of their "glam," still only get individuals to a certain level and no further.

The element of Water is obviously supposed to denote the fluid flowing, kind of, tidal ebb and flow, of qualities of existence. For most intents and purposes, we most often attribute that, again, to the emotional aspects of Self—because the element seems to denote the kind of—it's not as heavy as the Earth element, but it's certainly not as free and (dispersed) as the Air element.

And so in that respect, we consider the "emotional tides," of which certain physical—for example, physical rocks, the physical (in metaphor terms) "things" that we encounter, whether (they have) turbulence or other obstacles and challenges and stuff that we encounter, like the rocks and walls of the physical. And the Air that blows over it, which could denote the qualities of the Mind and thought and so forth. Both of these have a strong *pull* on the quality of the water—on the flow of the water—and so as an element we see it connected to more of the "love" and "friendship," "connectivity," "interpersonal relationships" and so forth—anything where things are interwoven and tend to have a lot of emotional charge to them. [*Laughs*].

This too is reflected in... I mean, it's semi-controversial, I guess—in terms of the sciences... but the [Dr.] Emoto's work in terms of the "Secret Messages of Water" and how they have the ability to be imprinted and so forth in their crystal forms.

In terms of the applications in "ritual magic," Water and the Moon and the feminine have all been very tightly corresponded, concerning again, not only the emotions, but on a physical level: the blood, hormones, neurotransmitters—basically, the biochemicals. And we treat the reactivity of the biochemical qualities of the Human Condition in Systemological "processing." But, at a "magical" level, it's just treated as, well, "they exist." [*Laughs.*]

In terms of objects—anything that involves water or liquids; I mean, it doesn't have to be a "witches' cauldron," but, you know: the chalice, the grail, the bowls—all these. Every tradition seems to have some representation of that, which of course, is also reflected in the qualities of the strong feminine, qualities of receptivity and so forth. So, we see that a lot.

Also, anything involving water directly—whether it's the weather, in terms of like, rain; anything involving bodies of water, and then of, course, also "mirrors. Originally lakes and ponds and pools were used as "magic mirrors," so those are all aspects of the Water Element.

And don't get me wrong—I'm just kind of blowing through this stuff; but you can look up these individual facets in your *Arcanum* and then also cross-reference, if you're doing more work with the "Druid School" material. Everything of which I am describing is explained within its own right. I'm just kind of giving you an overview of what to look for and how to kind of arrange a "magical curriculum" for either a "Magic School" or "Druid School" or even Shamanism or whatever. We're moving into the Earth-oriented or Nature-oriented part of the "Master Course," so this is applicable to a lot of different areas.

And just like what you were doing with the solidity of the Earth Element and the... basically, the gravity and thickness of that—you would do the same thing in projecting an imaginative exercise in directing the experience of Self as being in the center of an Infinite Ocean that—more than just the visualization, again, getting the facets of it and the other qualities we were talking about before: the coldness, the dampness—these qualities being actually created or sensed artificially; imagined into being by the individual.

And the individual should *know* that *they* are the one creating this mental imagery and sensations; has the ability to do so at will; the ability to know they are doing so; the ability to disperse such, because these aren't permanent states here that we are trying to put ourselves in—we're trying to demonstrate fluid considerations of point-of-view within each of the Elemental Realms. And this is actually something that is done as part of high-level initiations in various orders of ceremonial magic and high magick.

It's found on the "Chaldean Oracles of Zoroaster," where an individual is brought through to various directions of the Circle and, you know, presented with this "powerful imagery" of the "lustral waters which sprinkle and rain down and pour forth" and da-da-da-da; and they go down to the next one... you'll see this in some of the ritual texts that we explore in our materials here. But this is done intentionally as a way of redirecting—selectively directing attention and point-of-view of the initiate, of the Seeker, in these various states; and the demonstration to the Seeker that these things *can* be done at Will.

Now, in addition to what I'm relaying here—and I'm not saying that this is the end-all be-all of what you can find out on these subjects. *Arcanum* simply is a concise synthesis of basically the "common denominator" of it all, to provide a basic unification of wide-spanning subjects and paradigms and semantic views on this level of understanding, brought together into one.

Unfortunately, there aren't... if we are looking at it at a "Master-Course" level—if this were *just* "Magic School"; if this were *just* treating ritualism and ceremonialism as the end-all be-all, then we would go about it a different way. And I actually have—I've done that in the past and primarily in the 90's—and so forth; however, there just isn't a lot of other outside material that I can recommend that doesn't simply conflict with what we're trying to do farther down and bring this to higher grades and broader higher levels of realization and understanding.

A lot of that—so... you can definitely have—if you're running a Magic School—you can even have it treated as a *coven* or a Circle or a "working group" or what not, so long as the emphasis of it is still being directed to continue the Seeker up the *Pathway*.

Now, one of the things I could mention: now.. just kind of a fluke of discovery in terms of research: is in the mid-90's, I happened upon a work by Ed Fitch called *A Grimoire of Shadows*—and the back portion of it, I found the most interesting, practical and useful for my purposes, mainly pertaining to "magical training." And the arrangement of it seemed very peculiar to me, because it was very concise, very... but, it seemed to be wholly different from the *Wicca* and witchcraft and paganism that was being relayed throughout the first part portions of the book.

It took my all of, I think, the rest of that year—as I was doing other supplemental work and research, pretty intensely at the time—to come upon the source of that material. And I was quite surprised, because it's not as well known. It's a book called *Initiation Into Hermetics* by Franz Bardon.

And for all of the other mainstream and popular works and presentations and watered-down treatments that appear out there with large publishers—even for all that we've...—the high esteem that's given to such like Aleister Crowley and these other ones that have been more prolific in their writing or better marketed, that particular title [*Initiation Into Hermetics*] goes kind of unnoticed in terms of really how incredible to see something like that from—as old as it is... I believe it was written in the 40's, in German originally.

But, the only issue being—is that, if we're working towards the Master Course understanding, things that we've been able to push forth in our Systemology, things that have developed, you know, ever since the 1940's and 50's and our new developments in "New Thought," we want to always emphasize the Self, the Alpha-Spirit, the I-AM as the point-of-view Observer, and its ability to freely direct that projection of its point-of-view; because it moves its point-of-view into a beingness of whatever its treating.

So, at this point, yes, it's great—we're getting people out of physical bodies; but we don't want to make the emphasis on Astral Bodies. We've not explored as fully in the Systemology Society yet, as we plan to in terms of these Astral Bodies, but it seems like in their present state, and without being treated in some other way or cleared on some other channels or something, they aren't have a natural compulsive dependency at this juncture to fix onto other more physical bodies—they don't seem to be strong enough, necessarily, to hold on their own.

And the Astral Body is not the Self; is not the Alpha-Spirit Self at all. It's just another "body" that's not as concrete or material in terms of its communications with other concrete material in the Physical Universe.

So, a lot of times, rather than an emphasis on what we would treat as the Alpha-Spirit or the I-AM as Self—the actual I that is the individual—a lot of the upper-level work of these other paths, or these other traditions, seem to put the emphasis on, again, just a different body—on the Astral Body. And so that's something that we kind of steer a little bit away from in terms of our—at least at the Master-level work—until we can explore that a little more deeper in the Systemology Society.

So there are other exercises and work that you can do from the materials—for example, *Druid's Handbook* or *Elvenomicon* or *Merlyn's Complete Book of Druidism*—well, let's just kind of get through these last two elements here before the day is out.

Now, we have the Air element which is closely tied to the Mind, the intellect, the Mind-System—the Mental Plane, if you want to call it that—any of the faculties, vibrations, of the Mind. So, this operates, again, at a higher relative rate than what you see with the emotional realm and Water and the physical realm and Earth. In the Standard Model, you see it work up here to the Mind-System.

And of the stuff we're dealing with in terms of Mind-Tech today; Mind-Tech is primarily dealing with thought discipline and willpower. In upper-levels of Systemology, we're getting back into visualization and mental imagery—all of these are pretty much paramount to any effective work that you're doing. I don't care if it's ritual magic or meditations or Systemology processing—the "Mind" seems to be the common denominator there, in terms of mental faculties, the "Mind-System" being used *by* Self to basically control the body or interact with the body; interact with the Physical Universe *using* a body—it seems to boil back to the Mind.

What we're talking about here is communication... we're always talking about communication when we're talking about energy movement—but, communication with the flow of energies and circuits and various channels between Self, the Spiritual Self (Alpha-Spirit) *and* a "body" *using* the Mind-System.

The traditional tool when it comes to the Mind and it comes to the Air Element and it comes to the ability to direct thought *is* the "Magic Wand." And the Magic Wand is always represented as the extension *of* the Wizard or the Magician or the Priestess *in* the Physical Universe. So, it was using an object *of* the Physical Universe that was independent of the Self, which is then imbued *as* a representation or an extension of the Self, such as you would use a pointer stick like in education... well, I guess they don't really use that anymore. They probably have digital screens and things now; but in my day, when we were going to school, they'd have a long stick and *whack* and point it *there*.

So, that's where you're dealing with the Air. And in that respect what you would deal with—I mentioned it in relationship to "space" before—you would do the same thing in your visualizations with "space"; seeing the Airy space as just going infinitely in all directions.

This type of "space" that we are talking about is *not* the "dark space" that you see out there in "outer space" when you look up at the night sky. We're talking actually—a different planar level of "space" that's actually white; "white space." And we deal actually, in the "Druid's Cabala"—and we'll get into that, maybe tomorrow—we deal with that "White Space," that "White Plane" there.

And then, of course, Fire being a transformative element—definitely represents the ability of the Will, the strong power of the Will, which is an Alpha quality (a spiritual quality) to enact effects, to be the cause to enact an effect, *in* the Physical Universe to create changes and what not.

In ritual traditions, in magick and so forth, and in my universal tradition—because there is some discrepancy with magical tools and "elemental weapons"—but, I have always allocated the "blade" (any "bladed" object) as the Fire elemental tool; having a Wand to represent Air, and the Blade to represent Fire. I'm not really sure why the Golden Dawn gets those the other way around, but...

So, there you have some "basic elemental tech" to tide you over until we get into Druidism in our next lecture tomorrow.

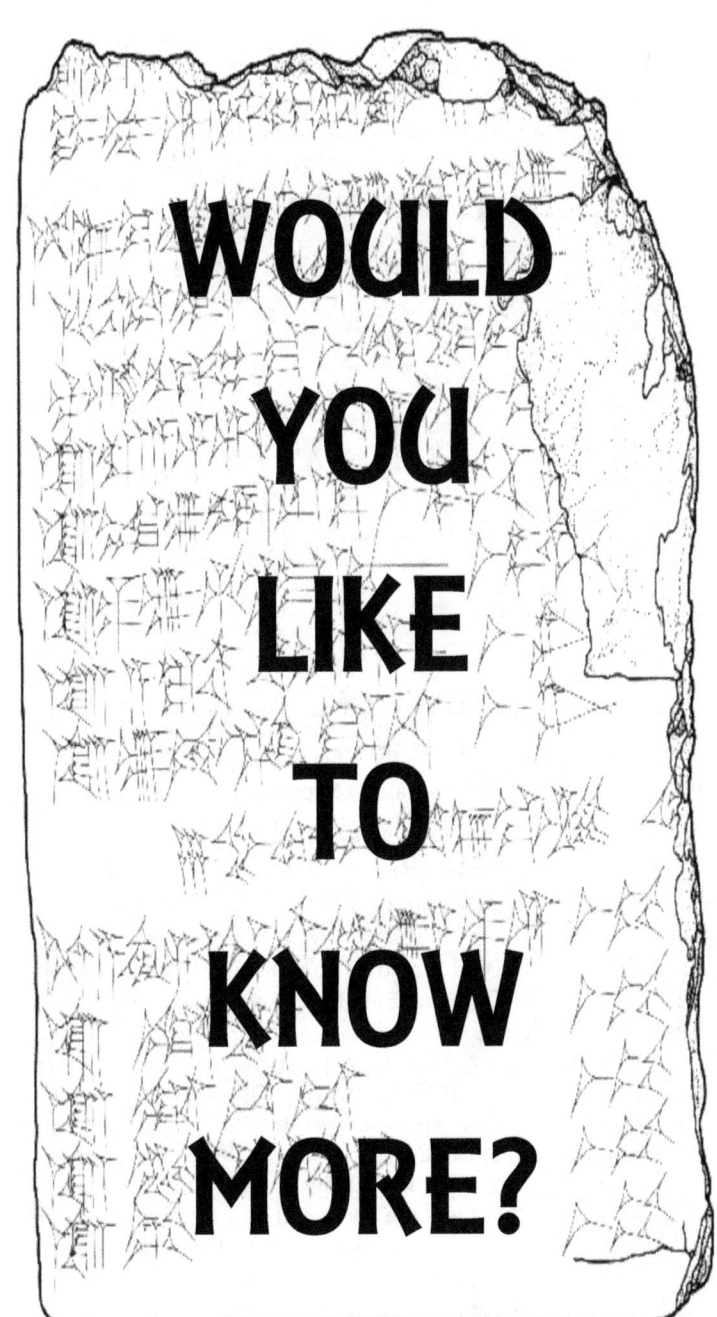

AVAILABLE FROM THE **JOSHUA FREE** PUBLISHING IMPRINT

The Original Classic Underground Bestseller Returns!
10th Anniversary Hardcover Collector's Edition.
Explore the original religion on Earth.

SUMERIAN RELIGION
Introducing the Anunnaki Gods
of Mesopotamian Neopaganism

by Joshua Free

Develop a personal relationship with Anunnaki Gods
—the divine pantheon that launched a thousand
cultures and traditions throughout the world!

Even if you think you already know all about the Sumerian Anunnaki or Star-Gates of Babylon... ✱ Here you will find a beautifully crafted journey that is unlike anything Humans have had the opportunity to experience for thousands of years... ✱ Here you will find a truly remarkable tome demonstrating a fresh new approach to modern Mesopotamian Neopaganism and spirituality... ✱ Here is a Master Key to the ancient mystic arts: true knowledge concerning the powers and entities that these arts are dedicated to... ✱ A working relationship with these powers directly... ✱ And wisdom to exist "alongside" the gods, ever to remain in the "favor" of Cosmic Law. The original precursor to *"Babylonian Myth & Magic."*

(*Mardukite Research, Grade-II Zuism, Liber-50*)

AVAILABLE FROM THE **JOSHUA FREE** PUBLISHING IMPRINT

THE COMPLETE BOOK OF MARDUK BY NABU

A Pocket Anunnaki Devotional Companion to Babylonian Rituals

edited by Joshua Free

10th Anniversary Collector's Edition Hardcover

Mardukite Liber-W Grade-II Zuism

THE MAQLU RITUAL BOOK

A Pocket Companion to Babylonian Exorcisms, Banishing Rites & Protective Spells

edited by Joshua Free

10th Anniversary Collector's Edition Hardcover

Mardukite Liber-M Grade-II Zuism

AVAILABLE FROM THE **JOSHUA FREE** PUBLISHING IMPRINT

SYSTEMOLOGY
The Pathway to Self-Honesty

A Basic Introduction to Mardukite Systemology

THE WAY INTO THE
FUTURE

A Handbook for the New Human

a collection of writings by
Joshua Free
as selected by James Thomas

now available as a Collector's Edition Hardcover

Here are the basic answers to what has held Humanity back from achieving its ultimate goals and unlocking the true power of the Spirit and highest state of Knowing and Being.

"The Way Into The Future" illuminates the *Pathway* leading to Planet Earth's true "metahuman" destiny. With *excerpts from "Tablets of Destiny," "Crystal Clear," "Systemology—Original Thesis"* and *"The Power of Zu."* You can help shine clear light on anyone's pathway!

Carefully selected by Mardukite Publications Officer, James Thomas, this critical *collection of eighteen articles, lecture transcripts and reference chapters* by Joshua Free is sure to be not only a treasured part of your personal library, but also the perfect introduction for all friends, family and loved ones.

(Basic Grade-III Introductory Pocket Anthology)

AVAILABLE FROM THE **JOSHUA FREE** PUBLISHING IMPRINT

SYSTEMOLOGY
The Pathway to Self-Honesty
ORIGINAL UNDERGROUND INTRODUCTIONS
REVISED AND REISSUED IN HARDCOVER

SYSTEMOLOGY
The Original Thesis of Mardukite New Thuoght
by Joshua Free
(*Mardukite Systemology Liber-S-1X*)

The very first underground discourses released to the "New Thought" division of the Mardukite Research Organization privately over a decade ago and providing the inspiration for rapid futurist spiritual technology called "Mardukite Systemology."

THE POWER OF ZU
Applying Mardukite Zuism & Systemology to Everyday Life
by Joshua Free
Foreword by Reed Penn
(*Mardukite Systemology Liber-S-1Z*)

A unique introductory course on Mardukite Zuism & Systemology, including transcripts from a 3-day lecture series given by Joshua Free in December 2019 to launch the Mardukite Academy of Systemology & Founding Church of Mardukite Zuism just in time for the 2020's.

AVAILABLE FROM THE **JOSHUA FREE** PUBLISHING IMPRINT

The Ultimate Necronomicon of the 21st Century!
Hardcover! Nearly 1000 Pages!

NECRONOMICON:
THE COMPLETE ANUNNAKI LEGACY
(*Complete Grade-II Master Edition Anthology*)
collected works by Joshua Free

And don't miss the newly released portable abridgment
of the original "Anunnaki Bible" scriptural edition...

ANUNNAKI BIBLE

THE CUNEIFORM SCRIPTURES
NEW STANDARD ZUIST EDITION

Premiere Founders Edition for
Church of Mardukite Zuism

edited by Joshua Free

Premiere Edition Hardcover
and
Pocket Paperback Available

WOULD YOU LIKE TO KNOW MORE ???

Take your first steps on the

SYSTEMOLOGY
Pathway to Self-Honesty

with the book that started it all!

Rediscover the original system of perfecting the Human Condition on a Pathway that leads to Infinity. Here is a way!—a map to chart spiritual potential and redefine the future of what it means to be human.

A landmark public debut of Grade-III Systemology and foundation stone for reaching higher and taking back control of your

DESTINY

(*Mardukite Systemology Grade-III Research Volume, Liber-One*)

AVAILABLE FROM THE **JOSHUA FREE** PUBLISHING IMPRINT

SYSTEMOLOGY
The Pathway to Self-Honesty

CRYSTAL CLEAR

The Self-Actualization Manual & Guide to Total Awareness

by Joshua Free
Foreword by Kyra Kaos

Mardukite Systemology
Grade-III, Liber-2B

*available in
Paperback and Hardcover*

Take control of your destiny and chart the first steps toward your own spiritual evolution.
Realize new potentials of the Human Condition with a Self-guiding handbook for Self-Processing toward Self-Actualization in Self-Honesty using actual techniques and training provided for the coveted "Mardukite Self-Defragmentation Course Program" —once only available directly and privately from the underground International Systemology Society.

Discover the amazing power behind the applied spiritual technology used for counseling and advisement in the Mardukite Zuism tradition.

AVAILABLE FROM THE **JOSHUA FREE** PUBLISHING IMPRINT

SYSTEMOLOGY
The Pathway to Self-Honesty

SYSTEMOLOGY HANDBOOK

*The ultimate operator's manual to the Human Condition
and unlocking the true power of the Spirit.*

** *"Modern Mardukite Zuism"* **
** *"The Tablets of Destiny"* **
** *"Crystal Clear"* **
** *"The Power of ZU"* **
** *"Systemology—Original Thesis"* **
** *Human, More Than Human* **
** *Defragmentation* **
** *Patterns & Cycles* **
** *Transhuman Generations* **

(Complete Grade-III Master Edition Anthology)

AVAILABLE FROM THE **JOSHUA FREE** PUBLISHING IMPRINT

MARDUKITE MASTER COURSE
Keys to the Gates of Higher Understanding

Now you can experience the Legendary "Master Course" from anywhere in the Universe, exactly as given in person by Joshua Free to the "Mardukite Academy of Systemology" in September 2020.

800+ pages of materials collected in this volume provide Seekers with full transcripts to all *48 Academy Lectures* of the legendary *"Mardukite Master Course"* combined with all course outlines, supplements and critical handouts from the original *"Instructor's Manual"*—making this the most complete definitive single-source delivery of New Age understanding and spiritual technology.

Referencing 25 years of research, development and publishing, including *"Necronomicon: The Complete Anunnaki Legacy," "The Great Magickal Arcanum," "The Systemology Handbook"* and *"Merlyn's Complete Book of Druidism."*

AVAILABLE FROM THE **JOSHUA FREE** PUBLISHING IMPRINT

SYSTEMOLOGY
The Gateways to Infinity

METAHUMAN DESTINATIONS

Piloting the Course to Homo Novus

Written by Joshua Free
Foreword by David Zibert

Mardukite Systemology Grade-IV Metahumanism Professional Pilot Course, Liber-Two

exclusively available in a hardcover premiere first edition

Drawing from the "Arcane Tablets" and nearly a year of additional research, experimentation and workshops since the introduction of applied spiritual technology and systematic processing methods, Joshua Free provides the ground-breaking manual for those seeking to correct—or "defragment"—the conditions that have trapped viewpoints of the Spirit into programming and encoding of the Human Condition.

Experience the revolutionary professional course in advanced spiritual technology for Mardukite Systemologists to "Pilot" the way to higher ideals that can free us from the Human Condition and return ultimate command and control of creation to the Spirit.

(Includes Grade-IV Liber-2C, Liber-2D and Liber-3C)

AVAILABLE FROM THE **JOSHUA FREE** PUBLISHING IMPRINT

SYSTEMOLOGY
The Gateways to Infinity

IMAGINOMICON

The Gateway to Higher Universes
A Grimoire for the Human Spirit

by Joshua Free

Mardukite Systemology Grade-IV Metahumanism, Wizard Level-0, Liber-3D

exclusively available in a hardcover premiere first edition

The Way Out. Hidden for 6,000 Years.
But now we've found the Key.
A grimore to summon and invoke, command and control, the most powerful spirit to ever exist.
Your Self.

Access beyond physical existence.
Fly free across all Gateways.
Go back to where it all began and reclaim that *personal universe* which the *Spirit* once called "*Home.*"

Break free from the Matrix;
command the Mind and control the Body
from outside those systems
— because *You* were never "human" —
fully realize what it means to be a *spiritual being*,
then rise up through the Gateways to Higher Universes
and *BE*.

AVAILABLE FROM THE **JOSHUA FREE** PUBLISHING IMPRINT

*Original underground classics.
Joshua Free's bestselling
"Druid Trilogy"*

DRACONOMICON
The Book of Ancient Dragon Magick
25th Anniversary Hardcover
Collector's Edition
by Joshua Free

THE DRUID'S HANDBOOK
Ancient Magick for a New Age
20th Anniversary Hardcover
Collector's Edition
by Joshua Free

ELVENOMICON -or- SECRET TRADITIONS OF ELVES AND FAERIES
The Book of Elven Magick
& Druid Lore
15th Anniversary Hardcover
Collector's Edition
by Joshua Free

*All three Grade-I Route-D titles
(...plus additional material...)
now available in the anthology:*

**Merlyn's Complete
Book of Druidism**
by Joshua Free.

AVAILABLE FROM THE **JOSHUA FREE** PUBLISHING IMPRINT

The Underground Occult Classics

Collector's Edition Hardcover now available for this 21st Anniversary Commemoration!

SORCERER'S HANDBOOK
A GUIDE TO PRACTICAL MAGICK
by Joshua Free writing as "Merlyn Stone"

And don't miss the never before published sequel from the 1990's originally released privately as "The 1998 Book of Shadows." A long-lost classic of 20th century wicca-witchcraft is alive again!

THE WITCH'S HANDBOOK
A COMPLETE GRIMOIRE OF WITCHCRAFT

Premiere Edition Hardcover

by Joshua Free writing as Merlyn Stone
edited and introduced by Rowen Gardner

THE MARDUKITE RESEARCH LIBRARY ARCHIVE COLLECTION

AVAILABLE FROM THE **JOSHUA FREE** PUBLISHING IMPRINT

Necronomicon: The Anunnaki Bible : 10th Anniversary Collector's
Edition—LIBER-N,L,G,9+W-M+S (*Hardcover*)

*Gates of the Necronomicon : The Secret Anunnaki Tradition of
Babylon :* 10th Anniversary Collector's Edition—
LIBER-50,51/52,R+555 (*Hardcover*)

*Necronomicon—The Anunnaki Grimoire : A Manual of Practical
Babylonian Magick :* 10th Anniversary Collector's Edition—
LIBER-E,W/Z,M+K (*Hardcover*)

The Complete Anunnaki Bible: A Source Book of Esoteric Archaeology
—LIBER-N,L,G,9+W-M+S (*Hardcover and Paperback*)

*Anunnaki Bible : The Cuneiform Scriptures—New Standard
Zuist Edition :* Abridged Pocket Version (*Hardcover & Paperback*)

*Sumerian Religion : Introducing the Anunnaki Gods of Mesopotamian
Neopaganism :* 10th Anniv. Collector's Ed.—LIBER-50 (*Hardcover*)

*Babylonian Myth & Magic : Anunnaki Mysticism of Mesopotamian
Neopaganism :* 10th Anniv. Coll. Ed.—LIBER-51+E (*Hardcover*)

*The Complete Book of Marduk by Nabu : A Pocket Anunnaki
Devotional Companion to Babylonian Prayers & Rituals :*
10th Anniversary Collector's Edition—LIBER-W+Z (*Hardcover*)

*The Maqlu Ritual Book : A Pocket Companion to Babylonian
Exorcisms, Banishing Rites & Protective Spells :*
10th Anniversary Collector's Edition—LIBER-M (*Hardcover*)

*Novem Portis: Necronomicon Revelations & Nine Gates of the Kingdom
of Shadows :* 10th Anniv. Collector's Ed.—LIBER-R+9 (*Hardcover*)

*Elvenomicon—or—Secret Traditions of Elves & Faeries : Elven Magick
& Druid Lore :* 15th Anniv. Collector's Ed.—LIBER-D (*Hardcover*)

Draconomicon : The Book of Ancient Dragon Magick
25th Anniversary Collector's Edition—LIBER-D3 (*Hardcover*)

The Druid's Handbook : Ancient Magick for a New Age
20th Anniversary Collector's Edition—LIBER-D2 (*Hardcover*)

The Sorcerer's Handbook : A Complete Guide to Practical Magick
21st Anniversary Collector's Edition—(*Hardcover*)

The Witch's Handbook : A Complete Grimoire of Witchcraft
21st Anniversary Collector's Edition—(*Hardcover*)

The Vampyre's Handbook : Secret Rites of Modern Vampires
5th Anniversary Collector's Edition—LIBER V1+V2 (*Hardcover*)

PUBLISHED BY THE **JOSHUA FREE** IMPRINT REPRESENTING

**The Founding Church of Mardukite Zuism
& Mardukite Academy of Systemology**

mardukite.com

www.ingramcontent.com/pod-product-compliance
Lightning Source LLC
Chambersburg PA
CBHW070313010526
44107CB00004B/325